Logos

This logo indicates a key point box, with tasks to do, tips and points to remember.

This logo indicates a listening exercise. Listen to your CD.

This logo indicates a reading exercise.

This logo indicates a writing exercise.

Et maintenant, au travail !

Contents

EDCO
FRENCH
REVISE WISE

JUNIOR CERTIFICATE HIGHER LEVEL

Geraldine McQuillan

Marie Stafford

Carmel Timmins

Edco
The Educational Company of Ireland

First published 2006
The Educational Company of Ireland
Ballymount Road
Walkinstown
Dublin 12

A member of the Smurfit Kappa Group

The
paper used in
this book comes
from Managed
Forests in
Northern
Europe
For
every
tree
felled, at
least one new
tree is planted

Proofreader: Isabelle Lemée and Juliette Péchenart
Illustrations: Philippe Tastet

PHILIPPE TASTET

Photos: Corbis and Shutterstock
Interior Design and Layout: Design Image
Cover Design: Combined Media
Cover Photo: Kenneth C. Zirkel/iStockphoto

Speakers: Clément Champion, Ludovic Degraeve, Haute-Claire Louis, Diane Mechani,
Florian Tessandier, Alix Verrando

Recorded at Trend Studios, Dublin

Texts: p. 52 *Pots de crème vanille-citron*, Femme Actuelle, n°1064, Aglaé Blin Gayet ; p. 56,
Christina Aguilera se fiance, L'Indépendant, 15 février 2005 ; p. 57, *Port-Vendres, Le maire
sortant présente sa liste*, L'Indépendant, 12 février 2005 ; p. 58, *Un bébé miraculé du tsunami
va retrouver ses parents*, L'Indépendant, 15 février 2005 ; p. 59, *Sournia, Marie Lamole a un
siècle !*, L'Indépendant, 12 février 2005 ; p. 60, *Nadège : 'Si Arturo l'avait exigé, j'aurais
arrêté la mode et la télé. Il a juste voulu un enfant.'*, Interview avec Céline Buanic, Paris
Match n°2460, Scoop ; p. 62, *Isild Le Besco : 20 ans, ni cigale ni fourmi*, Interview avec
Christine Haas, Paris Match n°2828, Scoop.

Section III: Written Expression   64

Revised

80 marks

Grammar   91

Revised

Exam Paper Analysis 2009   110

Revised

About this Book

The Main Sections

This book will help you to learn and practise progressively and effectively for your Junior Certificate Examination. You will find three chapters called **Listening Comprehension, Reading Comprehension** and **Written Expression**. Each of these chapters corresponds to the three sections of the examination paper. They contain lots of examples of the type of questions you will meet in your exam and tips on how best to prepare the answers.

In this book, you will also find:

- **Exercises** for you to do which mirror the type of questions appearing on the paper. This will mean you have lots of practice before the exam. In the **'Were you right?'** sections, you will be given the correct answers and an explanation.

- **Full Analysis of a recent Junior Cert. Paper**
  You will be guided through each section of the 2009 Higher Level paper and given suggested answers to each question. An explanation of each suggested answer is also given.

- **Vocabulary Revision Lists**
  These lists are set out topic by topic to help you increase your word power. They are referred to throughout the text.

- **Verb Table**
  This table outlines the five basic tenses needed for the Junior Certificate exam for the most common irregular verbs.

The Study Plan

This will help you to plan your work as you approach the examination. It can be used for daily or weekend revision.

How to use your Study Plan (see p. 167)
- **Fill** it in for each day or each weekend between now and the exam
- **Include** some listening, reading, vocabulary revision and written work
- **Do not fill** in more than you feel you will achieve
- **Set yourself** a fixed amount of time each day or each weekend to complete what you have set out to do
- **Tick off** each task as you complete it, which will help you track your progress
- **Start again** if you fall behind! Don't give up!

Introduction

The Junior Certificate French paper is divided into three sections:

	Listening Comprehension	Reading Comprehension	Written Expression	Total Marks awarded
Higher Level marks awarded	140	100	80	320

Getting started

- This is a **written examination**; the examiner can only judge what French you know by what you write down on the paper
- It is also a question of being able to **remember quite a lot of information**, such as vocabulary from your textbook or phrases your teacher has taught you. You need vocabulary for each section of the paper
- Get used to **writing for a long period of time**. You will have a lot of exams, one after another

Vocabulary

You need to be able to:

1   Recognise words from the **CD**
2   Recognise words from the **reading passages**
3   Use French words to complete the **written tasks**

Vocabulary Revision Lists

To help you with your vocabulary, use the **Vocabulary Revision Lists** (see pages 147-159). These are divided by **topic**. Many of the words are probably familiar to you from your own textbook, but having them organised topic by topic will make them easier to learn.

Set yourself a **realistic target**, e.g. **10 to 20 words each night**. When learning vocabulary involving nouns, make sure to **learn which gender** they are, i.e. '**le**' or '**la**', '**un**' or '**une**'.

Tips

- **Test yourself**: Cover the French words and try to **write** them
- Get **someone** at home **to help you**, by calling out the English word to see if you can **write** the French word
- You can also get a friend to help: **Quiz** each other on what you have learned, calling out words in English and trying to **write** the French word. Then reverse the process

Listening Comprehension

Examination Section

	Marks Available	% of Total Marks
Listening Comprehension	140 marks	43%

●●● Learning Objectives

1 **Experience** samples of each type of question
2 **Learn** keywords and phrases to deal with exam questions
3 **Practise** listening to exam questions using the CD
4 **Learn** how to write the best answers, by means of tip boxes
5 **Revise** phrases and words useful in the other parts of the paper

The examination step by step

● **Listen** to some French the evening before the exam
● On the day of the exam, make sure to arrive **on time**. If you are late, **you will not be allowed into the Exam Centre until the CD has finished** and you will have lost 140 marks

On your exam paper

● Remember to write all your answers in English. The rule is '**Questions in English, answers in English**', except for places and people's names, e.g. Jean, St Pierre-de-Bois
● **Underline the key question words**. This helps you to concentrate on the part of the CD where that particular answer occurs
● When you hear the CD for the **first time, just jot down notes** or shortened answers. Wait to hear it again, before writing your definite answer
● Where there is a **multiple-choice answer**, write only one letter in the box provided. Use capital letters, as this makes it easier for the correcting examiner to read:

B ✓   ~~a/c~~

● When the CD has finished take some time to go back over your answers. Write complete words and full answers

What Will I Hear?

The Listening Comprehension is the first part of the examination you will do. It will take approximately **30-35 minutes**.
There are five sections.

What will you hear in each section?

Section A Identify the conversation	Usually consists of **three short conversations**. You will be asked to identify what is happening in each conversation, or where the conversation is taking place. You will be given five suggestions to choose from. You will hear **each conversation twice**.
Section B Find personal details	Usually consists of **two people** talking about themselves. You will be asked to fill in a grid giving personal details, such as age, birthday, number in family, where they live, hobbies, holidays, likes and dislikes, etc. There is no pause until each person has finished speaking. You will hear **each person speak three times**.
Section C Find information	Usually consists of **five short conversations**. These may include someone shopping, someone making an appointment, someone asking directions, someone making a booking, etc. You will hear **each conversation twice**.
Section D Follow a conversation	Usually consists of **a longer conversation** between **two people**. They may be making plans for an outing, they may have met after a long time or they may have just returned from holidays. You will hear **the conversation three times**: Once right through with no pauses, secondly, with pauses between each part of the conversation and a third time right through the conversation again.
Section E News items	Usually consists of short **news items**. These may include reports of an accident, a sports event with the results and usually an item about the weather. You will hear **each news item twice**.

Remember...

1   Answer in **English**
2   Write your answers **clearly**
3   Attempt **every** answer
4   If the answer to a question is '**None**' or '**Nil**', be sure to indicate this.
    Do not leave a blank space! Write the word '**None**' or '**Nil**' or put a line through the box

Section A

How to deal with Section A

You will hear **three short conversations**. You have to identify what is happening in each conversation or where the conversation is taking place. You are given five suggestions, marked (a), (b), (c), (d) and (e). You will hear each conversation **twice**, with a short gap between each playing.

- **Read all the suggestions** first, so that you have some idea of what you are listening out for. Jot down any French keywords which you hope to hear
- **Listen** to the **tone of voice** used by the speakers. If they are complaining about something, they may sound angry. If they are not well, they may sound ill
- **Write your answer clearly** in the box provided. Remember that you can only make one suggestion

Topics of conversation

1	Making a booking	7	Making a complaint
2	Ordering a meal	8	Asking for or giving directions
3	Suggesting a meeting/outing	9	Saying you are not well
4	Cancelling an arrangement	10	Looking for something which is lost
5	Making an apology	11	Borrowing or lending something
6	Buying an item	12	Asking permission to do something

1 Making a booking

un **restaurant**/**hôtel**/**camping**	a restaurant/hotel/campsite
au **théâtre**	in the theatre
Je voudrais **réserver une table pour** deux personnes.	I would like to book a table for two.
Avez-vous **des chambres** pour… ?	Have you any rooms free for…?
Avez-vous **un emplacement de libre** ?	Have you any sites free?
Je voudrais **faire une réservation**…	I would like to make a booking…
… **pour vendredi soir**.	… for Friday night.
… **pour le 10 juin**.	… for 10 June.
… **pour la séance de** mercredi soir.	… for the show screening on Wednesday evening.
… **pour trois nuits**.	… for three nights.

To do!

Days or dates may be mentioned. From your **Vocabulary Revision Lists**, revise days and months, on page 149.

REVISE WISE
POINTS TO NOTE

2   Ordering a meal

une **entrée**/un **hors d'œuvre**	*starter*
un **plat principal**	*main course*
un **dessert**	*dessert*
une **boisson**	*drink*
Vous **désirez** ?	*What would you like?*
Voulez-vous **commander** ?	*Would you like to order?*
Oui, je **voudrais**…	*Yes, I would like…*
Est-ce que je peux avoir… ?	*May I have…?*
Je vais prendre…	*I am going to have…*

To do!

From your **Vocabulary Revision List**, on page 155, revise the names of food items.

REVISE WISE
POINTS TO NOTE

3   Making plans for meeting/an outing/an invitation

Allons au cinéma !	*Let's go to the cinema!*
Tu voudrais venir/aller... ?	*Would you like to come/go…?*
Ça te dit de venir… ?	*How about coming…?*
Je **t'invite à une boum**	*I'm inviting you to a party*
Rendez-vous à midi.	*Meeting at midday.*
Je **te verrai /retrouverai** à la gare	*I'll see/meet you at the station.*

4   Cancelling an arrangement

Désolé(e), mais je…	*Sorry, but I…*
Je ne peux pas.	*I can't.*
Malheureusement, je …	*Unfortunately, I…*
Je dois **annuler** notre rendez-vous.	*I have to cancel our appointment.*
Je serai de retour trop tard	*I'll be back too late.*

5   Making an apology

Je voudrais **faire mes excuses**.	*I would like to apologise.*
Je te téléphone pour **m'excuser**.	*I am phoning to apologise.*
Je **regrette**, mais je n'étais pas poli(e).	*Sorry, I was rude.*
Excusez-moi, je suis en retard.	*Sorry, I am late.*
Est-ce que tu peux **me pardonner** ?	*Can you forgive me?*
Pardon, Madame, j'ai raté l'autobus.	*Excuse me, Miss, I missed the bus.*
Je suis **désolé(e)**.	*I am sorry.*

6 Buying an item (see also 1, page 10)

In a shop/market

Je voudrais **acheter** …	*I would like to buy …*
Je peux **l'essayer** ?	*May I try it on?*
Je préfère le rouge / le bleu	*I prefer the red one / the blue one*
Il est trop grand / long / court	*It's too big / long / short*
Vous avez ce t-shirt en noir ?	*Do you have this t-shirt in black?*
Quelle taille ? / **Quelle pointure** ?	*What size? (clothes)* *What size? (shoes)*
Donnez-moi un kilo de …	*Give me a kilo of …*
Ils sont frais ?	*Are they fresh?*

To do!

From your **Vocabulary Revision Lists** revise words for quantities, on page 156.

REVISE WISE
POINTS TO NOTE

Ça **fait** combien ?	*How much does that come to?*
Ça **coûte** combien ?	*What does that cost?*
C'est pour **offrir** ?	*Is it a present?*
C'est un **cadeau** pour….	*It is a present for…*

In a railway/bus station (see also 8, page 14)

Je voudrais **un aller simple**.	*I would like a single ticket.*
un aller-retour	*a return ticket*
première/deuxième classe	*1st/2nd class*
fumeur/non-fumeur	*smoking/non-smoking*
côté couloir/côté fenêtre	*aisle seat/window seat*
N'oubliez pas de **composter** votre billet !	*Don't forget to stamp your ticket!*

In a post office (see also 2, page 11)

Je **voudrais** deux **timbres**.	*I would like two stamps.*
Je **voudrais** envoyer **une carte postale**.	*I would like to send a postcard.*
Je peux avoir un **mandat postal** ?	*May I have a postal order?*
Où est la **boîte aux lettres** ?	*Where is the post-box?*

Track 1 – You will hear this conversation **twice**.
In this conversation say whether someone is:
(a) making a booking; (b) cancelling a booking; (c) ordering a meal.

Tips

1   If it is (a), you will probably hear the word 'réserver'
2   If it is (b), you will probably hear the word 'annuler'
3   If it is (c), you will probably hear the word 'commander'

Were you right?

The first clue was when the woman says '**nous ne pourrons pas venir vendredi prochain**' (*we cannot come next Friday*). She then says 'Je dois **annuler** notre réservation' (*I have to cancel our booking*). She also adds 'Je suis **désolée**' (*I am sorry*). The manager then says '**j'annule** votre réservation'. So the answer is **(b)**.

Now listen to **Track 2** and check your answer on page 132.

Track 2 – You will hear this conversation **twice**.
In this conversation say whether someone is:
(a) buying something; (b) making an apology;
(c) suggesting an outing.

7   Making a complaint

Je voudrais **me plaindre** du/de la/des…	*I would like to complain about…*
Je suis **très déçu(e)**.	*I am extremely disappointed.*
Je demande un **remboursement**.	*I demand a refund.*
Je **ne suis pas satisfait(e)** de mon appareil photo.	*I am not satisfied with my camera.*

7

8   Asking for or giving directions

The main directions are: **à droite** (*to the right*);
à gauche (*to the left*); **tout droit** (*straight ahead*).

Je **cherche**…	*I am looking for…*
Où est la gare, s'il vous plaît ?	*Where is the station, please?*
Où **se trouve** le/la/les…	*Where is the …?*
Pour aller au/à la… ?	*How do I get to the…?*
Prenez la prochaine rue à gauche.	*Take the next street on the left.*
C'est **à droite/à gauche/tout droit.**	*It is on the right/left/straight ahead.*
Traversez/Tournez/Continuez	*Cross/Turn/Continue*
en face de/à côté de/au bout de/	*opposite/beside/at the end of/*
devant/derrière	*in front of/behind*

From your **Vocabulary Revision Lists**,
on pages 152/153, revise the names of main
buildings in a town and the names of shops.

9   Saying you are not well (see also 3, page 11 and 8, page 29)

Je **ne me sens pas** bien	*I don't feel well*
Je me sens **malade**.	*I feel sick.*
J'ai **mal au/à la/aux**…	*I have a pain in…*
Je voudrais aller **chez le docteur/**	*I'd like to go to the doctor/*
le dentiste	*dentist*
Ça me **fait mal**…	*That hurts me.*
C'est le cabinet de/du…?	*Is that the surgery of…?*
Je voudrais **prendre rendez-vous**.	*I would like to make an appointment.*
Je vous donne **une ordonnance**.	*I will give you a prescription.*
Vous avez quelque chose pour… ?	*Have you got something for…?*
Je voudrais **des comprimés pour**…	*I would like some tablets for…*
Où se trouve **la pharmacie**	*Where is the nearest chemist shop?*
la plus proche ?	

From your **Vocabulary Revision Lists**, on
page 148, revise the names of parts of the body.

10 Looking for something which is lost

Je **cherche**…	I am looking for…
Je **ne trouve pas** mes lunettes.	I can't find my glasses.
Est-ce que **tu as vu** mon sac ?	Have you seen my bag?
Où est/Où sont…?	Where is/Where are…?
J'ai **perdu** mon livre.	I have lost my book.
J'ai **égaré**…	I have mislaid…

11 Borrowing or lending something

TU PEUX ME PRÊTER…?

Tu peux me **prêter**… ?	Can you lend me…?
Peux-tu **me donner**… ?	Can you give me…?
Est-ce que je peux **emprunter**… ?	Can I borrow…?

12 Asking permission to do something

EST-CE QUE JE PEUX SORTIR ?

Est-ce que je peux **aller**… ?	Can I go…?
Puis-je… ?	May I…?
Est-ce que **j'ai la permission** de… ?	Do I have permission to…?
Pourrais-je… ?	Could I…?

Track 3 – You will hear this conversation **twice**.
In this conversation say whether it is about:
(a) buying something; (b) borrowing something;
(c) saying they are not well.

REVISE WISE POINTS TO NOTE

Tips

1	If it is (a), you will probably hear '**je voudrais**' – *I would like* (a price may be included)
2	If it is (b), listen out for the words '**emprunter**' (*borrow*) or '**prêter**' (*lend*)
3	If it is (c), listen out for '**malade**', '**je ne vais pas bien**', '**j'ai mal au/à la**…'

Were you right?

Did you hear the girl say: '**Je ne me sens pas bien, j'ai mal à la tête et à la gorge**' (*I don't feel well, I have a headache, my throat is sore*)? She also mentions '**me sentir mal**' (*not feeling well*). Her mother offers her '**une boisson chaude et de l'aspirine**' (*a hot drink and aspirin*). Answer: (**c**).

Now listen to **Track** 4 and check your answer on page 132.

Track 4 – You will hear this conversation **twice**.
In this conversation say whether it is about:
(a) asking permission to do something; (b) looking for a lost item; (c) cancelling an arrangement.

Another way of asking for information is to ask you to identify where a conversation is taking place. If you are asked to identify where a conversation takes place, listen carefully for keywords or phrases.

Keywords and phrases for places

Possible places might be:

1	Market or shop	6	Restaurant
2	Post office	7	Airport
3	Hospital/Doctor's surgery	8	Railway station
4	Tourist office	9	Police station
5	School	10	Service station

1   Market or shop (see also 6, page 6)

Je voudrais **un kilo de**…	*I would like a kilo of*…
un **litre de**…	*a litre of*…
un **paquet de**…	*a packet of*…
un **morceau de**…	*a piece of*…
une **paire de**…	*a pair of*…
une **bouteille de**…	*a bottle of*…
Ce sera tout ?	*Is that all?*
Et avec ça ?	*Anything else?*
Ça fait combien ?	*How much does that come to?*

Tips

Revise words for measurements from your **Vocabulary Revision Lists**, on page 156. Revise also the names of fruits, vegetables, grocery items and items of clothing, on pages 155 and 159.

2 Post Office (see also 6, page 6)

Je voudrais **envoyer**...	*I would like to send...*
Je voudrais... **timbres**.	*I would like... stamps, please.*
Une lettre pour l'Irlande,	*How much does it cost*
cela coûte combien ?	*to send a letter to Ireland?*

3 Hospital/Doctor's surgery (see also 9, page 8 and 8, page 29)

J'ai **mal** aux/à la...	*I have a pain in...*
Ça me fait mal.	*It is hurting me.*
Je voudrais **prendre**	*I'd like to make an*
un rendez-vous	*appointment*
Ça vous fait mal où ?	*Where does it hurt you?*
C'est **urgent** !	*It is urgent!*
J'ai besoin d'**une radio**.	*I need an X-ray.*
Où est **la salle des urgences** ?	*Where is the A and E?*
Voilà **une ordonnance**.	*Here is a prescription.*
Vous avez la **grippe**.	*You have got the flu.*
Vous avez de la **fièvre**.	*You have got a temperature.*
Ouvrez la **bouche**.	*Open your mouth.*
Je me suis **cassé/blessé/**	*I have broken/injured/*
foulé/brûlé/coupé.	*twisted/burnt/cut.*

To do!

From your **Vocabulary Revision Lists** on page 148, revise words for parts of body.

REVISE WISE
POINTS TO NOTE

4 Tourist office

Je cherche des **renseignements**.	*I am looking for information.*
Avez-vous **un plan** de la ville ?	*Have you got a map of the town?*
une carte de la région	*a map of the area*
une liste des hôtels	*a list of hotels*
À quelle heure ouvre/ferme le/la... ?	*When does the... open/close?*
Vous avez les **horaires** des trains/bus ?	*Do you have a train/bus timetable?*
Qu'est-ce qu'il y a **à faire** et **à voir** ici ?	*What is there to do and see here?*
Il y a des **excursions** à... ?	*Are there outings to...?*

5   School

Attention, je fais l'appel.	Pay attention, I am going to call the roll.
Prenez vos livres à la page dix.	Go to page ten of your books.
Ouvrez vos livres.	Open your books.
Sortez vos cahiers.	Take out your copies.
Écoutez/Écrivez/Lisez/Faites	Listen to/Write/Read/Do
Allez voir le directeur !	Go to the principal!
Tu auras deux heures de colle.	You will be in detention for two hours.
Tu aimes le nouveau prof de géo ?	Do you like the new geography teacher?
Notre prof d'anglais est très juste/sévère	Our English teacher is very fair/strict
Je ne trouve plus mon emploi du temps	I can't find my timetable.

To do!

From your **Vocabulary Revision Lists**, on page 150, revise words for school subjects.

REVISE WISE POINTS TO NOTE

6   Restaurant (see also 6, page 28)

Voici votre table Monsieur/Madame.	This is your table, sir/madam.
J'ai faim	I'm hungry
J'ai soif	I'm thirsty
Je voudrais voir la carte.	I would like to see the menu.
Je voudrais commander.	I would like to order.
Comme entrée je prendrai…	As a starter I will have…
Pour commencer je prendrai…	To start with I will have…
Comme plat principal…	For my main course…
un dessert	dessert
une boisson	drink
L'addition, s'il vous plaît !	The bill, please!
Garçon !	Waiter!

To do!

From your **Vocabulary Revision Lists**, on page 155, revise the names of food.

REVISE WISE POINTS TO NOTE

Track 5 – You will hear this conversation **twice**.
Say where this conversation is taking place:
(a) a post office; (b) a railway station; (c) a tourist office.

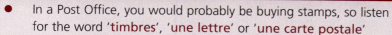

Tips

- In a Post Office, you would probably be buying stamps, so listen for the word 'timbres', 'une lettre' or 'une carte postale'
- In a Railway Station, you should recognise the words 'train', 'billet', 'aller-retour', 'aller simple', 'quai' or the phrases 'À quelle heure part…', 'C'est direct ?', 'Il faut changer de train ?'
- In a Tourist Office, you would hear words like : 'renseignements', 'une carte de la région', 'un plan de la ville', 'une liste d'hôtels, de campings, de monuments'

Were you right?

Did you hear the words '**envoyer une lettre en Irlande**' (*send a letter to Ireland*)? Both the woman and the girl used the word '**timbre**' (*postage stamp*). The person also asked if there was '**une boîte aux lettres**' (*a letter box*) near by. Answer: (**a**).

Now listen to **Track 6** and check your answer on page 132.

Track 6 – You will hear this conversation **twice**.
Say where this conversation is taking place:
(a) a restaurant; (b) a market; (c) a tourist office.

7 Airport

Je **prends l'avion pour**…	*I am taking the plane to…*
À quelle heure **part/arrive le vol**… ?	*At what time will the flight leave/arrive…?*
départ/arrivée	*departure/arrival*
Quelle porte pour **le vol** FR 936 ?	*Which gate for the flight FR 936?*
Il y aura **un retard** de vingt minutes.	*There will be a delay of twenty minutes.*
Je prends la **navette** pour l'**aérogare**.	*I am taking the coach for the air terminal.*
Les passagers sont priés de se rendre à la porte 2.	*Passengers are asked to go to gate 2.*

8   Railway station (see also 6, page 6)

À quelle heure **part le train pour**… ?	*What time does the train for… leave?*
Je voudrais **un aller simple**.	*I would like a single ticket.*
un aller-retour	*a return ticket*
compartiment **non-fumeur/fumeur**	*non-smoking/smoking compartment*
côté couloir/côté fenêtre	*aisle seat/window seat*
De quel **quai** part le train ?	*From which platform does the train leave?*
Est-ce que je dois **changer** de train ?	*Do I have to change?*
Le train **est-il direct** ?	*Is it a direct train?*
Où est **le buffet de la gare** ?	*Where is the station restaurant?*
N'oubliez pas de **composter votre billet** !	*Don't forget to stamp your ticket!*

9   Police station

Bonjour, **Monsieur l'agent** !	*Good morning, officer!*
J'ai **perdu** mon **passeport**.	*I have lost my passport.*
On m'a **volé** !	*I have been robbed!*
On m'a **agressé** !	*I have been attacked!*
Je voudrais signaler un accident.	*I would like to report an accident.*

10   Service station

faire **le plein d'essence**	*to fill up with petrol*
essence **sans plomb**	*unleaded petrol*
Pouvez-vous **vérifier les pneus** ?	*Can you check the tyres?*
Pouvez-vous **essuyer le pare-brise** ?	*Can you clean the windscreen?*
J'ai un **pneu crevé**.	*I have a flat tyre.*
Ma voiture est **en panne**.	*My car has broken down.*
Avez-vous **une dépanneuse** ?	*Do you have a tow-truck?*
C'est **le moteur/les freins/les phares**.	*It is the engine/the brakes/the headlights.*

Track 7 – You will hear this conversation **twice**.
Decide where this conversation is taking place:
(a) a tourist information office; (b) a market; (c) a railway station.

Tips

- Why do you go to a Tourist Information Office? To get 'des renseignements', a map 'une carte/un plan', a list of accommodation 'une liste d'hôtels/de campings/d'appartements à louer'
- What would you be doing in a market? Listen for: 'je voudrais/je désirerais…'; weights: 'un kilo/…grammes'; cost: 'euros, … centimes'
- Why go to a railway station?
  - To ask about trains: 'il y a un train pour… ?'
  - 'À quelle heure part le train pour… ?'
  - To buy a ticket : 'aller simple/aller-retour', '1ère/2ème classe'.
  - To ask where the train departs from: 'Quel quai ?'

Were you right?

The woman asked if there was a train 'le prochain train pour Bordeaux part à quelle heure ?'. She bought 'un aller-retour, 2ème classe' (*return ticket, second class*) and she asked where the train departed from, 'le train part de quel quai ?' Answer: **(c)**.

Now listen to **Track 8** and check your answer on page 132.

Track 8 – You will hear this conversation **twice**.
Decide where this conversation is taking place:
(a) a bank; (b) a petrol station; (c) a police-station.

Now continue to **Section B**.

Section B

How to deal with Section B

In Section B, you will hear two people speaking about themselves:

- One will be male and one female
- You will hear each conversation **three times**
- You will hear the entire conversation right through. You will get a **pause** at the end of each playing, during which you can **write down** your answers
- You will fill in your answers on a grid

Tips

- Underline the **keywords/phrases** first
- Do not stop to fill in the information on the first hearing. Just jot down notes for yourself
- You will hear more information than you need, so just listen out for the **keywords**
- Your **answers** must be given **in English**

Topics of conversation

The details will usually deal with personal facts about the person:

- Age, birthday, star sign
- Family details: brothers, sisters, parents, occupations
- Family home: location, size
- School: location, size, subjects liked or disliked, how the person travels there

- Hobbies/Pastimes
- Holidays: where, when, activities
- Pets
- Friends
- Career/Future plans

Track 9

You will hear **two** students introducing themselves, first Jérôme and then Florentine.

First Speaker – Jérôme Lejeune
Before you listen to Jérôme, read the **hints** below the grid.

Name	Jérôme Lejeune
1 His age	
2 Where he lives (**one** point)	
3 Number of sisters	
4 **Two** of his hobbies	(i)
	(ii)
5 Where he goes on holidays	
6 What he does while he is there (**one** point)	
7 His future career	

Hints

- ### His age
To find out somebody's age, listen carefully for a number and the word '**ans**':
seize ans *sixteen years old*

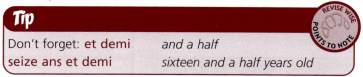

> **Tip**
> Don't forget: **et demi** *and a half*
> **seize ans et demi** *sixteen and a half years old*

REVISE WISE
POINTS TO NOTE

- ### Where he lives

Remember your words for dwellings:
une **maison**	*a house*
un **appartement**	*an apartment/flat*
un **pavillon** / une **maison individuelle**	*a detached house*
un **bungalow**	*a bungalow*
un **immeuble**	*a block of flats*
une **HLM**	*a council flat/house*
(Habitation à Loyer Modéré)

It may be:
en ville	*in town*
à la campagne	*in the country*
dans un village	*in a village*
dans la banlieue	*in the suburbs*
au bord de la mer	*beside the sea*
à la montagne	*in the mountains*
au 5 ième étage	*on the fifth floor*

- ### Number of sisters
The word for sister is '**sœur**', so listen out for this and a number. Be realistic, it would be unlikely to be '**douze sœurs**'!

- ## His hobbies

When you are asked for **two answers**, there are liable to be **three possibilities**. Listen for words such as '**faire du sport**' or the names of individual sports:

le basket	*basketball*	aller au cinéma	*to go to the cinema*
l'équitation	*horseriding*	la lecture/lire	*reading/to read*
le foot	*soccer*	écouter de la musique	*to listen to music*
la natation	*swimming*	jouer d'un instrument	*to play a musical instrument*
le rugby	*rugby*	regarder la télévision	*to watch TV*
le ski nautique	*water-skiing*	peindre/dessiner	*to paint/to draw*

To do!

Check for other sports/pastimes in the Vocabulary Revision Lists, on pages 152 and 158.

- ## Where he goes on holidays

en Espagne	*to/in Spain*	à la campagne	*in the country*
en Italie	*to/in Italy*	à l'étranger	*abroad*
en Irlande	*to/in Ireland*	au bord du lac	*at the lakeside*
aux États-Unis	*to/in the United States*	au bord de la mer	*at the seaside*
au Canada	*to/in Canada*	dans les montagnes	*in the mountains*
au sud/nord de…	*in the south/north of…*	chez mes	*to my*
à l'est/l'ouest de…	*in the east/west of…*	grands-parents	*grandparents'*
dans les Alpes	*in the Alps*		

To do!

Revise the names of other countries from your Vocabulary Revision Lists, page 157.

- ## What he does while he is there

This may depend on where he is staying. If he is at the seaside, it may be '**nager**' or '**faire de la voile**'. If he is in the country, it could be helping out on a farm ('**j'aide**'). If he is in the mountains, it might be '**faire du ski**', '**faire de l'escalade**'.

- ## His future career

The word for *career* is '**carrière**' or he might say '**métier**', which means *trade*. Do make sure you have revised all the names for careers/trades. Look at your **Vocabulary Revision Lists**, on pages 157/158, for this. He may say '**plus tard, j'aimerais être…**' (*later on I would like to be…*) or '**comme carrière, je choisirai celle de…**' (*as a career I will choose…*).

Now listen to **Track 9** and fill in the grid with details about Jérôme, on page 17. You will hear Jérôme **three times**.

Were you right?

- In the first sentence, Jérôme tells us he is '**seize ans**' (*16 years old*)
- He makes three points about where he lives. He says he lives in a '**maison individuelle**' (*a detached house*), '**au bord de la mer**' (*it is beside the sea*) and '**dans le Finistère**' (*in Finistère*). Any one of these points is sufficient for your answer
- Did you hear '**trois**' (*three*), when referring to his sisters?
- He says that because he lives beside the sea, he loves to sail ('**faire de la voile**'). Living beside the sea, should also help you to pick out his other two pastimes. He mentions '**je fais aussi de la natation et du ski nautique**' (*swimming and water-skiing*). You need to mention **two** of these to get your marks
- '**Vacances**' was the keyword to listen for. He says he often goes to visit his grandparents' farm in Normandy ('**je vais souvent chez mes grands-parents, en Normandie**. Ils ont une assez grande ferme...')
- Since he is on a farm, you need to think along the lines of what you might do on a farm. He says he spends a lot of time '**à aider mon grand-père...**' (*helping his granddad*) '**... avec les animaux**' (*with the animals*). He also mentions going *horse-riding* ('**je fais aussi de l'équitation**'). Either one of these activities is correct
- He says he would like to be a *vet* ('**j'aimerais devenir vétérinaire**'), because he loves animals

Track 10
Second Speaker – Florentine Rocher
Now read the **hints** concerning Florentine on page 20.

Name	Florentine Rocher
1 Her birthday	
2 Country where she was born	
3 Colour of eyes	
4 Colour of hair	
5 Musical instrument played by her	
6 **Two** subjects she likes at school	(i)
	(ii)
7 **One** animal she dislikes	

Hints

- ### Her birthday

To find out her birthday, you may hear the word '**anniversaire**' or '**je suis née le…**'. There will be a number (the date) and a month of the year. Don't worry if you don't get both points the first time you hear the conversation.

- ### Country where she was born

She will say '**Je suis née en/au…**'. As she is French-speaking, it may be a French-speaking country, such as **Belgique**, **Suisse**, **Luxembourg**, **Canada**, **Maroc…**

> **To do!**
>
> From your **Vocabulary Revision Lists**, on page 157, revise the names for countries

REVISE WISE POINTS TO NOTE

- ### Colour of eyes

j'ai les yeux	bleus	*blue eyes*	verts	*green eyes*
	marron	*chestnut/brown eyes*	gris	*grey eyes*
	bruns	*brown eyes*	sombres	*dark eyes*
	noisette	*hazel eyes*	clairs	*light eyes*

- ### Hair

Remember the various words for hair colour:

j'ai les cheveux	blonds	*fair hair*	noirs	*black hair*
	bruns	*brown hair*	roux	*red hair*

j'ai les cheveux	bouclés	*wavy*	courts	*short*
	frisés	*curly*	mi-longs	*mid-length*
	raides	*straight*	en brosse	*tight cut*
	une frange	*fringe*	en tresse	*plaits*
	longs	*long*	une queue de cheval	*pony-tail*

- ### Musical instruments played by her

What musical instruments do you know? **Piano**, **violon**, **guitare**, **flûte**, **clarinette**, **trompette**, etc. These all sound somewhat like their English counterparts. Watch out for **batterie** (*drums/percussion*) and **clavier** (*keyboard*).

● Subjects she likes at school

Since you are asked for **two** subjects, three will probably be mentioned in the conversation. *School subjects* (**matières**) will be something you will have revised from your **Vocabulary Revision Lists**, on page 150.

The words **préféré(e)** or **favori(te)** means *favourite*. She may say 'j'adore' or 'j'aime beaucoup'. Be careful: She may also include subjects she does not like. You may hear her say 'je déteste' or 'je n'aime pas'.

● One animal she dislikes

There may be more than one animal mentioned. What you need to find is the one where she says '**je déteste**' or '**je n'aime pas**'. What animals might one not like? Perhaps '**des souris**' (*mice*), '**des araignées**' (*spiders*), '**des serpents**' (*snakes*) or it might be one of the more usual domestic animals.

un chat	*a cat*	un poisson rouge	*a gold fish*
un cheval	*a horse*	un perroquet	*a parrot*
un chien	*a dog*	une perruche	*a budgie*
un cochon d'Inde	*a guinea pig*	un lapin	*a rabbit*
un hamster	*a hamster*	une tortue	*a tortoise/turtle*

Tip

You will find the names of other animals in your **Vocabulary Revision Lists**, on page 147.

 Now listen to **Track 10** and fill in the grid with details about Florentine. You will hear her **three times**.

Check your answers on page 133.

Now continue to **Section C**.

Section C
How to deal with Section C

- This section consists of **five short conversations**, each of which deals with a different topic
- Each conversation is a separate item, so you will hear it **twice** and then **no more**
- There are usually **two questions** for each conversation
- There will be a **gap after each playing** for you to answer the questions

Topics of conversation

1 Numbers
2 The French alphabet
3 Streets directions
4 Description of items
5 Booking a room or a campsite
6 Booking a table/Ordering a meal
7 Talking about school or a school event
8 Visiting the doctor/Making an appointment

1 Numbers

Phone numbers

French phone numbers consist of **ten** numbers, given in groups of **two digits**, e.g. 01.25.73.49.82. (zéro un, vingt-cinq, soixante-treize, quarante-neuf, quatre-vingt-deux). Mobile phone numbers in France start with 06.

Prices

Like ourselves, the French use the **euro**, but instead of the word cent, they use 'centime', e.g. €3.50 would be 'trois euros, cinquante centimes'.

€3.50

Try to be realistic in your answer. If the person is buying a kilo of apples, the price is unlikely to be €16! If the person is buying a shirt, he/she will not be paying €4.50.

Time

The French use the twenty-four hour clock, but you may give your answer in twelve hour or twenty-four hour form, e.g. if you hear 'seize heures trente', you can write 16.30 or 4.30 or 'half past four', and you will get the marks for your answer.

16:30

Locations

The number of someone's house: '**numéro dix-huit**'; the floor: something is '**au huitième étage**'; which turn to take: '**la troisième rue**'.

Sizes

When buying shoes or clothes you will hear numbers. '**Quelle pointure ?**' is used for shoe sizes. '**Quelle taille ?**' is for clothing like jumpers, skirts, jackets, shirts, etc.

Page/Exercise numbers

You might be asked the exercise and page number of somebody's homework: '**Faites l'exercice quatre, page quatre-vingt-douze**'.

Quantities

Someone buying petrol, for example, might ask for '**vingt litres d'essence**', or someone in a bakery might ask for '**six croissants**'.

> **Remember...**
>
> Words such as '**une douzaine**' (*a dozen*), '**une quinzaine**' (*a fortnight*), '**une centaine**' (*about one hundred*) could be heard.

Track 11 – Listen to the following **numbers**. They may be prices, times, phone numbers or locations. There are ten short sentences and each one contains a number or numbers. You will hear each sentence **twice**. Check your answers on page 133.

2 The French alphabet

This occurs as:

- Spelling someone's name: '**nom de famille**' (*surname*) or '**prénom**' (*first name*)
- Spelling the name of a town or location

> **Tip**
>
> The main difference in the sound of the French and English alphabet occurs in the vowel sounds. The letters **g**, **h**, **j** and **y** are also pronounced differently.

Track 12 – Listen to the vowels as they are pronounced **three times** in French.

Track 13 – Now listen to the consonants as they are pronounced **three times** in French.

Track 14 – Listen to these people spelling their names or the town where they live. There are six examples.

You will hear each example **twice**.

Check your answers on page 133.

3   Street directions

When you hear the conversation first, you may not be able to write everything down. Some people find it helps to draw out the instructions, e.g. if someone says '**allez tout droit et c'est la troisième rue à gauche**'.

← 3rd left

Tip

Listen to the verbs mentioned: **tournez, allez, continuez, prenez, traversez**, etc.

Or, you might write: straight, 3rd l.

Prepositions

Revise your **prepositions**, which tell you where something is situated:

en face de	*facing, opposite*	le long de	*along the*
devant	*in front of*	au bout de	*at the end of*
derrière	*behind*	près de	*near the*
à côté de	*beside*	entre	*between*

How is the person travelling?

à pied/je marche	*on foot*	à vélo	*by bicycle*
en voiture	*by car*	à moto	*by motorcycle*
en bus	*by bus*	**en** train	*by train*

You will find the names of other vehicles in your **Vocabulary Revision Lists**, on page 159.

To do!

Revise all the names of public buildings that you might find in a town, **Vocabulary Revision Lists**, pages 152/153.

Track 15, Conversation 1 – You will hear this conversation **twice**. Listen to the conversation and note down where the person wants to go to, and the directions given in order to get there.

Were you right?

Did you hear the word '**piscine**' (*swimming-pool*)? Keywords for the directions were: '**tout droit**' (*straight ahead*); '**deuxième**' (*second*); '**à gauche**' (*to the left*); '**à côté du cinéma**' (*beside the cinema*).

 Now listen to **Track 15, Conversations 2 and 3**. Check your answers on page 134. Note where the person wants to go and the directions given. You will hear each conversation **twice**.

4 Description of items

Something might be lost or mislaid. What sort of items get lost or mislaid?

List of items

mon portefeuille	*my wallet*	mes clés	*my keys*
mon porte-monnaie	*my purse*	mon carnet d'adresses	*my address book*
mon argent	*my money*	mon billet d'avion	*my plane ticket*
ma montre	*my watch*	mes chaussures de sport	*my sports shoes*
mon parapluie	*my umbrella*	mes boucles d'oreilles	*my earrings*
mon blouson	*my jacket*	mon passeport	*my passport*
mon K-Way	*my rainjacket*	mon portable	*my mobile phone*
mon bracelet	*my bracelet*	mon sac	*my bag*
mon appareil photo numérique	*my digital camera*	mon chargeur de téléphone	*my phone charger*

You are sometimes asked to describe the item. This involves revising your **adjectives** or describing words such as:

Size

grand(e)	*large, big*	énorme	*huge*	carré(e)	*square*	large	*wide*
petit(e)	*small*	minuscule	*tiny*	rond(e)	*round*	gros	*big (fat)*

Material

en or	*gold*	en coton	*cotton*
en argent	*silver*	en laine	*woollen*
en bronze	*bronze*	en plastique	*plastic*
en cuir	*leather*	en soie	*silk*

To do!

Use your **Vocabulary Revision Lists** on page 148 to revise your colours.

Condition

nouveau/nouvelle	*new*	avec mon nom	*with my name*
tout(e) neuf(ve)	*brand new*	sur la couverture	*on the cover*
usé(e)	*worn*	à l'intérieur	*on the inside*
avec une inscription	*with an inscription*	à l'extérieur	*on the outside*

Track 16 – You will hear each conversation **twice**.
Listen to these short conversations, with descriptions of articles which are lost or mislaid. There are five conversations. Listen to the first conversation and write what has been lost and its description.

Were you right?

The girl can't find '**mes baskets neuves**' (*my new trainers*). They are '**noires et blanches**' (*black and white*).

Now listen to the other **four conversations** and check your answers on page 134.

5 Booking a room or campsite

What type of room?

une chambre pour une personne	*single room*
une chambre avec deux lits	*twin room*
une chambre double	*double room*
une chambre pour une famille	*family room*

What type of site?

un emplacement pour une tente	*site for a tent*
un emplacement pour une caravane avec voiture	*site for a caravan and car*

What facilities?

avec salle de bains	*with a bathroom*	au rez-de-chaussée	*on the ground-floor*
avec douche	*with a shower*	à l'ombre	*in the shade*
avec balcon	*with a balcony*	avec l'électricité	*with electricity*
avec vue sur la mer	*with a view of the sea*	avec le gaz/l'eau	*with gas/water*

For how many people?

| pour deux personnes | *for two* | pour ma famille | *for my family* |
| pour ma femme et moi | *for my wife and myself* | pour deux adultes | *for two adults* |

For how long?

c'est pour une nuit	*for one night*	une quinzaine	*a fortnight*
deux nuits	*two nights*	le week-end	*the weekend*
une semaine	*a week*	un mois	*a month*

When?

| pour ce soir | *for tonight* | du quatre au six novembre | *from 4 until 6 November* |
| pour lundi | *for Monday* | pour le mois de juillet | *for July* |

What type of booking?

| en pension complète | *full board* | avec petit-déjeuner | *with breakfast* |
| en demi-pension | *half-board* | | |

Track 17, Conversation 1 – You will hear this conversation **twice**. Listen to this woman who is booking accommodation. Note (a) what type of room/site she requires; (b) what facilities she would like; (c) when she needs the booking for.

Were you right?

The woman wanted '**une chambre** pour deux nuits' (*one room*). She would like a room with '**douche**' (*a shower*) and '**vue sur la mer**' (*a sea view*). The dates she gives are '**du trois au cinq novembre**' (*from 3 to 5 November*). This reinforces that she wants the accommodation for two nights.

Now listen to **Track 17, Conversations 2 and 3**. You will hear each conversation **twice**. Check your answers on page 134.

Conversation 2	Conversation 3
(a) How many rooms?	(a) Type of site?
(b) For how many people?	(b) How many people?
(c) What dates?	(c) When needed?

27

6   Booking a table/Ordering a meal (see also 6, page 12)

This may involve:

Mentioning a day or date:	*C'est pour lundi le 6.*
Why you want the table:	*C'est l'anniversaire de mon mari.*
How many people are coming:	*C'est pour trois personnes.*
At what time:	*À huit heures et demie.*
Where your table is:	*Juste à côté de la fenêtre/sur la terrasse/en face de…*
Ordering a meal:	*Je voudrais commander/prendre…*
Asking for the bill:	*L'addition, s'il vous plaît !*

To do!

Revise words for food (page 155), your numbers (page 147) and days of the week (page 149) from your **Vocabulary Revision Lists**.

REVISE WISE POINTS TO NOTE

Track 18, Conversation 1 – You will hear this conversation **twice**. (a) For how many people is the reservation made; (b) for when; (c) what is the occasion?

Were you right?

In the first conversation the woman mentions (a) '**une table pour deux personnes**' (*a table for two*); (b) '**pour jeudi prochain, le quatre mars**' (*next Thursday, 4 March*); (c) After the reservation has been confirmed the woman adds '**c'est l'anniversaire de ma grand-mère**' (*it is my grandmother's birthday*).

Now listen to **Track 18, Conversation 2** and note the same information as you did for Conversation 1. Check your answers on page 135.

Track 19, Conversation 1 – You will hear this conversation **twice**. Listen to the conversation and note what the two people order for starters, main course, dessert and drinks.

Were you right?

- As '**entrée**' (*starter*), the woman chooses '**le potage du jour**' (*soup of the day*). Her partner picks '**une salade de tomates**' (*tomato salad*)
- For '**plat principal**' (*main course*), the man asks for '**l'agneau**' (*the lamb*) and the woman picks '**le saumon**' (*the salmon*)
- To drink '**comme boisson**' they have '**une bouteille de vin blanc**' (*a bottle of white wine*) and '**une carafe d'eau**' (*a jug of water*)
- The desserts chosen are '**un sorbet au citron**' (*a lemon sorbet*) and '**la mousse au chocolat**' (*chocolate mousse*)
- The waiter repeated the order at the end of the conversation, which should help you to fill any gaps you may have had

Now listen to **Track 19, Conversation 2**. You will hear this conversation **twice**. Write down what is ordered. Check your answers on page 135.

7 Talking about school or a school event

- You may have to listen out for a school subject: revise these from your **Vocabulary Revision Lists**, on page 150
- You may hear why someone was not at school: **il/elle est malade/en retard/en vacances…**
- You may have to listen for an exercise or page number: **page dix, exercice trois, la liste de vocabulaire…**
- Someone may be having problems with a school subject/with a teacher: **je suis nul(le) en…, je ne comprends pas, je trouve cette matière difficile, j'ai de mauvais rapports avec…**

Track 20, Conversation 1 – Listen to these three people talking about school life. In each case say, (a) what subject is mentioned; (b) what comment is made. There are three short conversations.

Were you right?

They were talking about '**l'épreuve de géo**'. He had studied all about '**l'Allemagne**' (*Germany*) and the words '**climat, industries, rivières, montagnes**' should have helped you to realise it was a Geography test they were talking about. The words '**bonne note**' may also have helped you to guess that it was a test.

Now listen to **Track 20, Conversations 2 and 3**. You will hear each conversation **twice**. In each case say, (a) what subject is mentioned; (b) what comment is made. Check your answers on page 136.

8 Visiting the doctor/Making an appointment (see also 3, page 11)

- You may have to listen for a day or time. Revise the days of the week from your **Vocabulary Revision Lists**, page 149.
- You may have to listen for an ailment
- You may have to listen for the doctor's advice

Gardez le lit deux jours !	*Stay in bed for two days!*
Allez à la pharmacie/à l'hôpital !	*Go to the chemist/hospital!*
Prenez ces antibiotiques/comprimés !	*Take these antibiotics/pills!*
Buvez beaucoup !	*Drink lots!*
Ne mangez rien !	*Don't eat anything!*
N'allez pas au soleil pendant cinq jours !	*Stay out of the sun for five days!*
Portez un chapeau au soleil !	*Wear a hat in the sun!*

Track 21, Conversation 1 – You will hear each conversation **twice**. Listen to this person discussing his health problems with the doctor. What is the complaint, how long has the patient had the symptoms and what is the advice given?

Were you right?

The patient says 'j'ai mal au ventre' and 'j'ai vomi' (*stomach-ache* and *vomiting*). 'Depuis deux jours' (*it has been going on for two days*). The doctor advises to 'boire beaucoup' (*drink lots*) and 'ne pas manger' (*not to eat*). You can sometimes use your own common sense about the advice a doctor might give. The doctor also says, 'si vous n'allez pas bien d'ici 24 heures' (*if you are not better in 24 hours*) 'téléphonez-moi' (*phone me*). Then the doctor will give 'une ordonnance' (*a prescription*).

Now listen to **Track 21, Conversations** 2 and 3. You will hear each conversation **twice**.

Fill your answers on the grid below.

Conversation 2	Conversation 3
Complaint:	Complaint:
Symptoms:	How long:
Doctors advice: (i) (ii) (iii)	Appointment for:

Check your answers on page 136.

Now continue to **Section D**.

Section D
How to deal with Section D

- Section D consists of a **longer conversation**
- There are **two people**, usually one male and one female, or one person and a group (2005)
- You will hear this conversation **three times**:
  The **first time**, it will be played from beginning to end without a pause. The **second time**, it will be played in segments or sections. You will see this clearly marked on your examination sheet. There will be a pause to allow you answer the questions in that segment/section. The **third time**, the conversation will be played right through again.

Remember...

- Do not be put off by the length of the conversation. You do not have to note every single thing that is mentioned
- **Read through the heading**: It will usually tell you the circumstances of the conversation, e.g. *Jean-Paul and Maryse meet after their holidays in Ireland*
- Read through the English questions for each section/segment. This should further help you to deal with the gist of the conversation
- During the **first playing** of the conversation, do not try to answer the questions. You could jot down notes for yourself
- When the conversation is played the **second time**, you should get ready to write your answers
- There are usually two or, at the most, three questions in each segment. The pause will be sufficient for you to write most, if not all, of your answer
- When you hear the conversation for the **third and final time**, try to complete any blank spaces you may have left or complete any answers you may not have had time to finish

Track 22 – You will now hear a conversation between Arnaud and Mélanie who have not seen each other for some time. You will hear this conversation **three times**.

First, you will hear it all right through without pauses. Then, it will be replayed in **four segments** with pauses. Finally, you will hear the whole conversation right through again.

First Segment

1 Where has Arnaud been for the past six months?
2 What has he been doing there?
3 When did he get back?

Second Segment

4   What has Mélanie been doing in the meantime?
5   Why did she choose to do this?
6   Why is she in a hurry now?

Third Segment

7   What does Arnaud suggest?
8   Why does this not suit Mélanie?
9   What alternative is suggested?

Fourth Segment

10   Where is Arnaud going now?
11   Why is he going there? (**one** reason)

Hints

First Segment

From the introduction we know that Arnaud has been away for the past while; Arnaud and Mélanie have not seen each other for six months. So you need to listen out for the name of a country or city/town. What was he doing there? He could have been *studying* (**j'étudiais**), or *working* (**je travaillais**), or *travelling* (**je voyageais**). When did he get back? Sometime recently, or Mélanie would have met him already. So listen out for 'il y a…' (… *ago*).

Second Segment

What has Mélanie done in the meantime? We know they last met after the examinations. Maybe she has been *studying* or *working* (**j'étudiais, je travaillais**). Why did she choose this? Listen carefully to what she says when Arnaud says '**Pourquoi est-ce que tu as choisi ça ?**' Why is she in a hurry? Does she mention a time? Does she have to go somewhere now?

Third Segment

Arnaud says he wants to tell Mélanie about his experiences, so what do you think he suggests? Are they going to meet? When? Where? We know this doesn't suit Mélanie (Question 8). She must be doing something else at the time. Try to imagine what this might be. What time of day had been suggested? This might give you a clue. Question 9 asks what the alternative arrangement is (maybe another day or time is suggested).

Fourth Segment

Where is Arnaud going now? Listen out for the name of a place, maybe a building or a shop. Why is he going there? This will depend on the place concerned. So getting the answer to Question 10 may be the key to the answer to Question 11.

Now listen to **Track 22** and answer questions 1 to 11 on pages 31 and 32. Check your answers on pages 136/137.
Now continue to **Section E.**

Section E
How to deal with Section E

- This section consists of **five short news items**, each of which deals with a different topic, e.g. an accident, a sports report, a weather report
- Each item is separate, so you will **hear it twice** and then **no more**. **Listen** carefully to each item
- There are usually **two questions** for each item
- There will be a **gap** after each playing for you to answer the questions
- Be aware of major news items/sports events concerning France. This might help

Tips

- **Read** the questions carefully. Underline **key question words** such as 'Who', 'When', 'Why', etc.
- **Jot down** your answers as you listen. Do not write the full answer until you have a gap in the conversation

Topics of conversation

1   An accident
2   Robbery/Theft
3   Natural disasters
4   Sports reports
5   Weather reports

1   An accident

un **accident**	*an accident*
une **collision**	*a collision*
entrer en **collision** avec	*to collide with*
percuter	*to crash/strike*
frapper	*to strike*
écraser	*to crash into/smash*
renverser	*to overturn*

What vehicles were involved?

To do!

Revise the names for vehicles from your **Vocabulary Revision Lists**, page 159.

33

When did the accident take place?

hier	*yesterday*
hier soir	*yesterday evening*
il y a deux jours	*two days ago*
jeudi dernier	*last Thursday*

The outcome

Someone could be:

grièvement/sévèrement **blessé(e)**	*seriously injured*
légèrement **blessé(e)**	*slightly injured*
transporté(e) à l'hôpital	*brought to hospital*
tué(e)/mort(e)/choqué(e)	*killed/dead/shocked*
la route était **bloquée/fermée**.	*the road was blocked/closed*
le conducteur **a été arrêté**	*the driver was arrested*
elle a dû **payer une amende**	*she had to pay a fine*

What was the cause?

Il faisait **noir**.	*It was dark.*
Il y avait du **brouillard**.	*There was fog.*
Il y avait du **vent**/du **verglas**.	*It was windy/icy.*
La route était **dangereuse/glissante**.	*The road was dangerous/slippy.*
Le conducteur **roulait trop vite**.	*The driver was going too fast.*
Le cycliste ne faisait pas **attention**.	*The cyclist wasn't paying attention.*
Le camionneur **ne s'est pas arrêté** aux **feux**.	*The lorry driver didn't stop at the lights.*
Il/Elle a essayé de **dépasser**.	*He/she was trying to overtake.*
Il/Elle téléphonait sur son **portable**.	*He/she was talking on his/her mobile phone.*

Someone could have been to blame

Le conducteur **roulait trop vite**.	*The driver was going too fast.*
Il/Elle ne s'est pas arrêté(e) au **feu rouge**.	*He/She didn't stop at the red light.*
Le cycliste ne faisait pas **attention**.	*The cyclist didn't pay attention.*

Track 23, News item 1 – You will hear this report **twice**. Note (a) what vehicles were involved; (b) the possible cause of the accident; (c) what happened to the young boy.

Were you right?

It was an 'accident routier' (*a road accident*). There were two means of transport mentioned: 'un poids lourd' (*a truck*) and 'vélo' (*a bicycle*). The cause was 'la route était glissante' (*the road was slippy*), because of 'verglas' (*ice*). The cyclist was *brought to hospital*, 'transporté à l'hôpital', but his condition is 'pas grave' (*not serious*). The truck driver was said to be 'en état de choc' (*shocked*).

Now listen to **Track 23**, **News items 2 and 3**. You will hear each report **twice** and answer the following questions.

News item 2: (a) How many vehicles were involved; (b) how were the injured brought to the hospital; (c) what was the possible cause?

News item 3: (a) Name the two vehicles involved; (b) who helped at the accident; (c) how long was the road blocked for?

Check your answers on page 137.

2   Robbery/Theft

un cambriolage	*house break in/robbery*
un vol	*theft*
un voleur	*a thief*

When did the incident take place?

hier	*yesterday*	mercredi dernier	*last Wednesday*
lundi dernier	*last Monday*	pendant la nuit de…	*during the night of…*

Where?

au centre de…	*in the centre of…*	dans un centre commercial	*in a shopping centre*
dans la ville de…	*in the town of…*	à la banque	*at the bank*
dans une grande surface	*in a shopping mall*	dans une bijouterie	*in a jewellers*

What was stolen?

des ordinateurs	*computers*	des bijoux	*jewels*
des milliers de…	*thousands of*	de l'argent	*money*
des portables	*mobile phones*	une voiture	*a car*

How did the criminals get away?

à moto	*by/on a motorcycle*	en camionnette	*by/in a van*
en voiture	*by/in a car*	à pied	*on foot*
en camion	*by/in a lorry*		

Track 24, News item 1 – You will hear this report **twice**. Listen to this report of a robbery. Note (a) when it happened; (b) what was stolen; (c) how the criminals made their escape.

Were you right?

The incident happened '**pendant la nuit de dimanche**' (*on Sunday night*). It concerned two robbers who entered a bank. You can probably presume that they stole money, in fact, €*10,000* ('**dix mille euros**'). Remember '**mille**' is a thousand, not a million! The police think they got away ('**pris la fuite**') in '**un vieux camion rouge**' (*an old, red lorry*).

 Now listen to **Track 24, News items 2 and 3**. In each case note, (a) when the robbery occurred; (b) what was stolen; (c) how the criminals got away. Check your answers on page 137.

3   Natural disasters

What occurred?

une sécheresse	*a drought*	une marée noire	*an oil-slick*
un orage/une tempête	*a storm*	une avalanche	*an avalanche*
une inondation	*a flood*	un raz-de-marée	*a tsunami*
un feu/un incendie	*a fire*	un tremblement de terre	*an earthquake*
un ouragan	*a hurricane*		

What people were affected/involved?

les habitants	*inhabitants*	les agriculteurs	*farmers*
les victimes	*victims*	les sapeurs-pompiers	*firemen*
les citoyens	*citizens*	les policiers/gendarmes	*policemen*
les résidents	*residents*	les vieux	*old people*
les riverains	*riverside residents*	les malades	*sick people*

What happened?

évacués/sauvés	*evacuated/saved*
blessés/morts	*injured/dead*
transportés à l'hôpital	*brought to hospital*
le village était détruit	*the village was destroyed*
les maisons étaient inondées	*the houses were flooded*
les animaux ont péri	*the animals perished*
la récolte était détruite	*the crops were destroyed*
la forêt était incendiée	*the forest was burnt out*
la route était bloquée	*the road was blocked*

Track 25, News item 1 – You will hear this report **twice**.
Listen to this news report of a disaster which has taken place recently in France. Note (a) the event which occurred; (b) when it occurred; (c) the outcome.

Were you right?

This news report referred to flooding. The keywords were '**deux jours de pluie**' (*two days of rain*). It occurred '**mardi et mercredi derniers**' (*last Tuesday and Wednesday*). The result of the heavy rain was that '**beaucoup de maisons ... sont inondées**' (*lots of houses are flooded*) and '**les habitants ont dû être évacués**' (*the people had to be evacuated*).

Now listen to **Track 25, News items 2 and 3**. You will hear each report **twice**.
Answer the following questions.

Item 2: (a) What crops were damaged? (b) how strong was the wind? (c) what is the estimated cost of the damage?

Item 3: (a) In what month is this taking place? (b) where is there a risk of fire? (c) what is now forbidden?

Check your answers on page 138.

4   Sports reports

Quite often you are asked for the results of sports encounters.

To do!

REVISE WISE
POINTS TO NOTE

From your **Vocabulary Revision Lists** on page 158 revise the names for sports. You may also need to know the French names of countries – see your **Vocabulary Revision Lists** on page 157.

Who was the winner?

a battu	*beat*
a vaincu	*defeated*
avait du succès	*was successful*
a gagné	*won*
a remporté le titre	*carried off the title*

Who lost?

a perdu	*lost*
a été vaincu(e)	*was defeated*
a été battu(e)	*was beaten*

What event?

le tournoi	*the tournament*	une course	*a race*
le championnat	*the championship*	une partie de	*a game of*
les Jeux Olympiques	*the Olympic Games*	un concours	*a competition*
la Coupe du Monde	*the World Cup*	la demi-finale	*the semi-final*

Track 26, News item 1 – You will hear this report **twice**. Listen to the following sports report and say (a) which sport is being spoken about; (b) who won the match; (c) what the score was.

Were you right?

Besides mentioning the word '**rugby**', the words '**Tournoi des Six Nations**' (*6-Nations Tournament*) might have helped you. The two teams involved were '**l'équipe écossaise**' (*the Scottish team*) – did you hear '*Murrayfield*'? – and '**l'Italie**' (*Italy*). What score? Scotland scored '**trente**' (*30 points*) and Italy '**quinze**' (*15 points*).

 Now listen to **Track 26, Conversations 2 and 3** and say (a) which sport is being spoken about; (b) who won the match; and (c) what the score was. You can check your answers on page 138. You will hear each report **twice**.

5   Weather reports

You need to be able to recognise the various areas in France

le Nord	the north	la Côte d'Azur	the Côte d'Azur
le Sud	the south	la Côte Atlantique	the Atlantic coast
l'Est	the east	le centre	the centre
l'Ouest	the west	la Côte Méditerranéenne	the Mediterranean coast
le Midi	the south of France	la Normandie	Normandy
les Alpes	the Alps	la Bretagne	Brittany
les Pyrénées	the Pyrenees	la Corse	Corsica

You may be asked to choose from a list of various weather types. These will be given to you in English. So you need to revise all the main types of weather. Use your **Vocabulary Revision Lists** on page 158. Sometimes you are asked for the weather forecast *for tomorrow* or *for the coming weekend* (listen out for the words '**demain**' or '**le week-end prochain**').

Track 27 – Listen to the following three weather forecasts. You will hear each one **twice**.

Forecast 1: (i) From the list of words below, select the word which best describes the weather in France.
Cold – Warm – Snow showers – Fog
(ii)   What temperatures are forecast?
(iii)   Outlook for tomorrow: _____

Were you right?

The first point made was '**il fera très chaud**' (*it will be very warm*). The fact that the temperatures were between '**23–30 degrés**' may have helped you with this answer. The words '**soleil**' (*sun*) and '**ensoleillé**' (*sunny*) were also mentioned in the forecast. The outlook for tomorrow was '**le beau temps continuera**' (*the fine weather will continue*).

 Now listen to **Track 27, Forecasts 2 and 3**. You will hear each forecast **twice**.

Forecast 2: (i) From the list of words below, select the word which best describes the weather in each of the parts of France mentioned.
Northern France:
Sunshine – Rain – Fog – Wind
Mountain region:
Rain – Fog – Snow – Frost
(ii)   Outlook for tomorrow: _____

Forecast 3: (i) From the list of words below, select the word which best describes the weather on the Atlantic coast of France
Mist – Cloudy – Strong winds – Ice
(ii)   Maximum temperature expected: _____

Check your answers on pages 138 and 139.

What next?

When you have finished the Listening Comprehension section
- Take a few minutes to read back over your answers to this section
- Complete sentences, where you left them unfinished
- Write out words in full, where you left shortened versions
- Make sure all your answers can be clearly read by the examiner
- Make sure you have left no gaps in your answers

You are now ready to move on to the Reading Comprehension section of the examination paper. It should be approximately 10:10 am and you still have one hour and fifty minutes left to complete your examination.

Reading Comprehension

Examination Section

	Marks Available	% of Total Marks
Reading Comprehension	100 marks	32%

●●● Learning Objectives

1 **Understand** articles from French magazines
2 **Understand** signs in public places
3 **Comprehend** information in French
4 **Extract** information from French ads, recipes, brochures, leaflets

The examination step by step

- There are 9–10 texts on the paper. You should spend about **one hour** on this section. All the **answers must be in English**
- In the longer extracts, the paragraphs are numbered and you are told in what section to find the answer
- In the longer extracts, you will find the answers in sequence – that is you move from part 1 to part 2 and so on

On your exam paper

- Read the **title** and any other information that may be given in English
- **Read the questions** first so that you know what to look for in the text
- Underline **key question words**, e.g. <u>why</u>, <u>where</u>, <u>how</u>, <u>when</u>
- Try to find the **meaning of words** by seeing if they look like the English word, e.g. *hôpital* means hospital, *vétérinaire* means a vet
- If you see the **circonflexe accent** (ˆ), try putting the letter 's' in its place and this will often give you the meaning of the word in English, e.g. *hôte* = host (this doesn't work all the time!)
- See if you can **add any more information** if the answer appears short
- Make sure you have taken the answers from the **correct part** of the text
- Check any **unanswered questions** and, before you finish, **try again**

What Will I Read?
What will I read in each section?

Question 1 Signs	There are **two questions**. You will be asked to pick the correct answer from a choice of four suggestions. Know all the **vocabulary for signs**. The signs are taken from roadsides, campsites, supermarkets, town centres and, recently, websites have appeared on the paper
Questions 2, 3, 4 Short reading pieces	These pieces are usually **quite short** and are taken from **French magazines/newspapers**. They concern food, houses, health, books or news items. These questions may also involve recipes, information leaflets or advertisements for restaurants, hotels, etc.
Questions 5, 6, 7, 8 Articles	These **articles are longer** than the previous reading pieces, **with more questions**. They concern **local news items** about people, events, crimes, sport, DVDs, film and book reviews, advertisements.
Questions 9/10 Long articles	This is **a long piece**, usually an **interview** with a French singer, actor or sportsperson. It is **divided into several parts**. You need to make sure that you have found the answer in the correct part of the text (you will be told where to look). There are usually **8 to 10 questions**.

Remember...

1 Answer all questions in **English**
2 Give as much **information** as possible
3 **Write clearly** so that the examiner can easily read your answers. You cannot get marks if the answer is not clear
4 When answering **multiple-choice questions**, put the answer in the box, because if not, you will not get any marks. Write in **capital letters** as they are easier to read

REVISE WISE
POINTS TO NOTE

To do!
Try to learn **10 new words of vocabulary** every night.

REVISE WISE
POINTS TO NOTE

Question 1

How to deal with Question 1

- Question 1 deals with **signs/advertisements/texts**. You must be able to match signs or choose the right sign, for example, if you want to buy a certain item, find a certain website or place, etc.
- Question 1 will have **two parts**: **(a)** and **(b)**

Here are some questions that have come up on Junior Cert. Papers

Question 1 – Exercise 1

(a) You are in a campsite in France and you want to find the Games room. Which sign would you follow?

(a) | Salle de jeux

(b) | Sortie

(c) | Piscine

(d) | Douches

Tips

You have enough time to think out your answer, so **don't rush** and always look at each of the four suggested answers. If you are not sure try a process of **elimination**; cross out what you are sure is **not** the answer!

Were you right?

- Look at *(a)*, '**Salle de jeux**': You will remember that the word '**salle**' means *room*. So *(a)* could give you the answer. But, before you decide, it is also a good idea to think about the other possible answers
- Look at *(b)*, '**Sortie**': You may remember that this means *exit*
- Now have a look at *(c)*, '**Piscine**': It means *swimming pool*
- So, you are left with *(d)*, '**Douches**': It means *showers*. If you didn't remember what that word meant, it is more likely that *(a)* is the correct answer, as '**salle**' means *room*
- You may also remember the expression '**jeux vidéo**', and deduce that the word '**jeux**' means *games*

(b) You are looking for an internet site to help you with your project on the climate of France. Which website would you choose?

(a) | www.cuisine.fr

(b) | www.franceautos.fr

(c) | www.météo.fr

(d) | www.chansons.fr

Check your answer on page 139.

Were you right?

- When you look at the websites you will see that *(a)* is to do with cooking, as you recognise the word '**cuisine**'. You know this can't be the answer
- Next look at *(b)* and you will see the word '**autos**' meaning *cars*, so you can see that this is not the answer either
- Now you are left with *(c)* and *(d)* so you have to make a decision between the two. The word '**météo**' looks like the English word *meteorology*. Maybe you know this word from your Geography class; it concerns the weather. You may also have heard of Met Éireann which provides you with the weather forecasts
- All this helps you to find the answer. You could make a good guess now and go for *(c)*, even though you don't know what *(d)* means ('**chanson**' means *song*)!

Road Signs

ROUTE GLISSANTE

Here is a list of signs that you should learn for this first part of the Reading Section. The list includes signs from past Junior Cert and past Mock papers.

la déviation	*diversion*	une route bis	*alternative road*
le sens unique	*one way*	une sortie de camions	*truck exit*
les travaux	*roadworks*	un stationnement interdit*	*no parking*
le péage	*toll bridge/road*	vous n'avez pas la priorité	*give way*
une voie sans issue	*cul de sac*	une aire de repos	*rest area*
sauf riverains	*local access only*	direction... Paris	*direction... Paris*
autres directions	*other routes*	... Vallée de la Loire	*direction... Loire valley*
toutes directions	*all routes*	... la plage	*direction... of the beach*
la station service	*service station*	la déchetterie	*rubbish dump*

*interdit = *forbidden/not allowed*

Here are some more questions

- Remember to look out for words that may be like English words
- Use a process of elimination, i.e. rule out the obviously **incorrect** answers

Question 1 – Exercise 2

(a) Your mobile phone has been stolen while you are on holiday in France, and you want to report the theft. Which sign do you follow?

(a) | Pompiers
(b) | Stade
(c) | Gendarmerie
(d) | Gare

> **Remember...**
> **Question 1** will have **2 parts**, **(a)** and **(b)**, and the question will involve recognising **signs** that you see in public places such as airports, roads, towns, shops, markets, parks, etc.

(b) Your parents want to find a pancake restaurant for lunch. Which sign should they look for?

(a) Buffet de la gare   *(c)* Restaurant chinois

(b) Musée   *(d)* Crêperie

Check your answers on page 139.

Railway station signs

la consigne	*lockers*
le buffet de la gare	*station restaurant*
le guichet	*ticket desk*
les renseignements	*information*
la salle d'attente	*waiting room*
la sortie	*exit*
l'entrée	*entrance*
défense de fumer	*no smoking*
l'accès aux quais	*access to platforms*
le bureau des objets trouvés	*lost property office*
côté couloir	*aisle seat*
fumeur	*smoking*

côté fenêtre *window seat*
non-fumeur *non-smoking*

> **To do!**
> From your **Vocabulary Revision Lists**, revise related words on page 151.

Town signs (shops and places)

la librairie	*bookshop*
la pâtisserie	*cake shop*
la boulangerie	*bakery*
la boucherie	*butchers*
l'hôtel de ville	*town hall*
le terrain de boules	*bowling green*
la papeterie	*stationery shop*
la mairie	*town hall*
la pharmacie	*chemist*
l'épicerie	*grocery*
la bibliothèque	*library*
les meubles	*furniture*
la maison de la presse	*news agent*
le syndicat d'initiative	*tourist office*
la crêperie	*pancake café*
le coiffeur	*hairdressers*
le musée	*museum*
le tabac	*tobacconist*
la quincaillerie	*hardware*
la confiserie	*sweetshop*

la gare SNCF	*train station*
la gare routière	*bus station*
l'aéroport	*airport*
la gendarmerie	*the police station*
l'église	*church*
location de vélos	*bicycle hire*
location de bateaux	*boat hire*
location de voitures	*car hire*
le stade	*stadium*

Signs inside a shop/supermarket

la fromagerie	*cheese*
les chaussures	*shoes*
les légumes	*vegetables*
la charcuterie	*delicatessen*
le rez-de-chaussée	*ground floor*
les produits laitiers	*dairy products*
l'ascenseur	*lift*
la sortie de secours	*fire exit*
la poissonnerie	*fish stall*
les boissons fraîches	*fresh drinks*
les soldes	*sale*
le premier étage	*first floor*
le sous-sol	*basement*
les vêtements	*clothes*

To do!

See your Vocabulary Revision Lists on page 153.

REVISE WISE
POINTS TO NOTE

School signs

le laboratoire de langues	*language lab.*
le gardien	*caretaker*
l'infirmerie	*sick bay*
le secrétariat	*office area*
le bureau	*office*
la sortie de secours	*fire exit*
la cantine	*canteen*
la salle des professeurs	*staffroom*
la salle de classe/cours	*classroom*
la salle d'informatique	*computer room*

Website/Internet sites

www.jardin.fr	*gardens*
www.motos.fr	*motorbikes*
www.bricolage.fr	*D.I.Y.*
www.cuisine.fr	*cooking/recipes*
www.mode.fr	*fashion*
www.autos.fr	*cars*
www.maison.fr	*house*
www.météo.fr	*weather forecasts*

Campsite signs

l'accueil	*reception*	terrain de sports	*playing field*
la salle de jeux	*games room*	une laverie	*laundry room*
les plats à emporter	*take away food*	une alimentation	*foodshop*
l'eau potable	*drinking water*	le bloc sanitaire	*toilets/showers*
les douches	*showers*	location de…..	*…..for hire*

Market stall signs

vend lapins	*rabbits for sale*
achète disques	*records wanted*
produits biologiques	*organic produce*
volaille de la ferme	*farm fresh poultry*
articles artisanaux	*handcrafted goods*
meubles d'occasion	*secondhand furniture*
vêtements d'occasion	*secondhand clothes*

Other signs to learn

gratuit(e)	*free of charge*
libre service	*self service*

Questions 2, 3 and 4

How to deal with Questions 2, 3 and 4

In the next part of the Reading section, you will see ads, menus, recipes, newspaper articles, magazine extracts, leaflets and brochures.

- You will have to answer two or three questions on each piece. These are Why, How, When, Where type of questions
- You will need to know vocabulary for food, days of the week, months, numbers, times of the day

> **To do!**
>
> REVISE WISE
> POINTS TO NOTE
>
> Make sure to revise vocabulary for food, holidays, sports, school, animals, etc., in your Vocabulary Revision Lists.

Faux amis

A lot of words in French look like English words and this is a great help in answering this section of the paper. These words include restaurant, chat, table, dîner, neveu, nièce, etc. However, some French words that look like English words do not have the same meaning. These words are called faux amis (*false friends*)!

Here is a list for you to learn:

location	*hire*	sensible	*sensitive*
une serviette	*a towel*	la pub	*advertising*
rester	*to stay*	un anniversaire	*a birthday*
un spectacle	*a show*	une note	*a mark in a school test*
un car	*a coach*	la lecture	*reading (the activity)*
une librairie	*a bookshop*	une nappe	*a tablecloth*
une pile	*a battery*		

Opening and closing times

There are often questions asking for opening times or closing times. You need to know these two keywords: **ouvert** (*open*) and **fermé** (*closed*).

You may see information like this:

Ouvert tous les jours…	*Open everyday…*
… <u>sauf</u> le mercredi	*… except on Wednesday*
Ouvert de 9h00 à 18h00.	*Open from 9 until 6 o'clock.*
Ouvert toute l'année.	*Open all year.*
Fermé le dimanche.	*Closed on Sunday.*
Fermé de 12h00 à 14h00.	*Closed from 12 to 2 o'clock.*

Here are some exercises

Question 2 – Exercise 1

Paintball
Le sport du 21ᵉᵐᵉ siècle !

Un loisir pour tous les âges !

Saison touristique :
Ouvert tous les jours

Hors saison touristique :
Ouvert les week-ends et sur réservation la semaine

3 sessions par jour :
10/12h – 15h/17h – 18/20h
En dehors de ces horaires, nous contacter.

(a) For what age group is this activity?
(b) When is the site open during the tourist season?
(c) When is the site open outside the tourist season?

Check your answers on page 139.

Question 2 – Exercise 2

Château La Chapelle
Horaires

Fin mars/avril/mai/juin Septembre/mi-octobre	10h00 à 18h00
Juillet/août	9h30 à 19h00
Fin octobre Début novembre	10h00 à 17h30

Fermé le samedi matin de 10h à 14h en mars, avril, oct. et nov.

(a) When is the castle open at 9.30 in the morning?

(b) On what day of the week is the castle closed in the morning during March, April, October and November?

Check your answers on pages 139.

Menus/Recipes/Articles on food/Healthy eating

 Question 3 – Exercise 1
Here is a recipe for a cake. The question asks you to find out from the list which ingredient is **not** included.

GÂTEAU FÊTE

- 1 génoise prête à l'emploi
- 1 sachet de sucre vanillé
- 100 g de sucre en poudre
- 500 g de poires
- 150 g de chocolat
- 30 cl de lait
- 10 cl de crème fraîche
- 10 cl de café fort
- 2 feuilles de gélatine

Which of the following is **not listed** in the ingredients?

(a) fresh cream

(b) chocolate

(c) flour

(d) pears

Were you right?

Don't try to work out all the words. Read the question first and then read the list to find the answer. Start with:

(a) 'crème fraîche': this is in the list. 'Crème' is an easy word to understand

(b) Move on to *chocolate*: this word is 'chocolat' in French, so it is easy to see if it is in the list or not

(c) The next word is 'farine' in French. Even if you don't know it, you can still work out the answer by finding the next word in the list

(d) Now you only have one option left. Even if you are not sure what the word 'poires' means, it looks like *pears* so you can see that in the list

By eliminating (a), (b) and (d), you are able to answer (c) correctly, even though you may not have known the word.

Recipes

ajoutez	*add*
beurrez	*butter/grease*
chauffer	*to heat/warm*
coupez	*cut*
couvrez	*cover*
épluchez	*peel*
lavez	*wash*
mélangez	*mix*
mettez au frigo	*put in the fridge*
poivrez	*put pepper on*
préchauffez le four	*preheat the oven*
salez	*put salt on*
servez chaud/froid	*serve warm/cold*
temps de cuisson	*cooking time*

Tips!

Revise words for ingredients and measurements in your **Vocabulary Revision Lists**, on pages 155 and 156.

Recipes may have the following words used for measurements:

1 cuillerée à café de…	*This is the French way of saying a teaspoon! So be careful you don't think that coffee is in the recipe!*
1 cuillerée à soupe de…	*This is the French way of saying a tablespoon.*
1 litre/1 demi-litre de… 250 g de…	*The recipes will have metric measurements so you won't see pounds and ounces.*

Expect to see recipes, newspaper articles, small ads, articles from magazines and newspapers. You may also see brochures from campsites and clubs. Here are some for you to try:

Question 3 – Exercise 2
Here is a brochure for a holiday village. Read it and answer the questions that follow.

> ## Village Vacances
>
> *Un village tout confort dans un cadre naturel et paisible.*
>
> *Au cœur du Périgord Noir, ses sites, grottes, villages, musées, châteaux, jardins.*
>
> *Piscine, volley, badminton, pétanque, jeux enfants, ping-pong... Snack...*
>
> *Ambiance conviviale pour de vraies vacances en famille...*

(a) Which one of these four is **not** on the list of things to see in the Périgord Noir region?

(a) museums	*(c)* windmills		
(b) castles	*(d)* caves		

(b) There are several activities on offer in the village. Name **two** of these activities, apart from volleyball and badminton.

_____

_____

(c) For which groups of people is this holiday village suited?

_____

Check your answers on page 139.

Question 3 – Exercise 3

Pots de crème vanille-citron

Pour 4 personnes – Préparation : 20 min
Cuisson : 35 min – Attente : 15 min + 2h

- **40 cl de lait entier**
- **1 gousse de vanille**
- **1 citron non traité**
- **4 jaunes d'œufs**
- **80 g de sucre**

- Préchauffez le four sur thermostat 5 (150°C).
- Rincez et séchez le citron. Prélevez le zeste sans entamer la peau blanche.
- Dans une casserole, portez le lait à ébullition avec la gousse de vanille fendue en deux dans la longueur et le zeste du citron. Retirez du feu, couvrez et laissez infuser 15 min. Faites bouillir à nouveau le lait parfumé.
- Dans une jatte, fouettez les jaunes d'œufs avec le sucre, jusqu'à ce que le mélange blanchisse et double de volume. Versez peu à peu le lait bouillant, en filet, sans cesser de fouetter. Filtrez à travers une passoire fine. Laissez reposer 5 min.
- Pour éviter les projections d'eau dans les crèmes, placez une feuille de papier sulfurisé dans le fond du plat à mettre au four. Pratiquez quelques encoches et disposez sur les quatre ramequins. Remplissez-les de la préparation vanille-citron. Versez de l'eau frémissante dans le plat, à mi-hauteur des ramequins. Placez au four et laissez cuire 35 min.
- Retirez les crèmes du bain-marie. Laissez-les refroidir, puis placez-les au réfrigérateur 2h minimum.
- Servez les crèmes directement dans les ramequins après les avoir décorées d'un zeste de citron.

Aglaé Blin Gayet, *Femme Actuelle*, n° 1064

(a) What fruit is needed for this recipe?

_____

(b) How long does it take to cook this dish?

_____

(c) In the second last point after you have taken them out of the cooking dish, what are you told to do with the desserts at this stage? **One** point

_____

Check your answers on page 139.

Question 4 – Exercise 1

Read the following ads for holiday rentals in the South of France.

4/5 pièces   Beaulieu sur Mer

Dans un grand immeuble, 140 m².
Étage élevé. Grand séjour, salle à manger,
cuisine, 3 grandes chambres, 1 salle de bains.
Charme. Balcons. Vue mer.

4/5 pièces   Vence

Une villa au centre ville. 200 m²
d'exception dans une demeure
bourgeoise sur jardin sud de 600 m².
Entrée privée par jardin. Garages.

5 pièces   Nice Ville

Proche Médecin, 122 m² environ
(divisible en deux), bourgeois, 3ème étage,
proche toutes commodités.

5 pièces   St. Laurent du Var

Dans un bel immeuble récent.
Appartement/Villa 5 pièces, 117 m² avec
beau jardin arboré de 200 m². Très belle vue
mer. Cuisine équipée. Arrosage
automatique. Cellier. Garage.

5 pièces   Antibes

Superbe duplex de 155 m² dans parc. Séjour,
4 grandes chambres. Terrasse,
vue sur mer, piscine, cave, garage.
Excellent état.

5 pièces   Cannes

Proche Promenade.
Beau 5 pièces, 120 m², parfait état, double
exposition, dans un immeuble début du
siècle. À voir.

5 pièces   Villefranche

Appartement de grand standing.
Près de la plage. 2 ème étage,
balcon 2 faces. Climatisé. Parking privé.

Write the name of the town where there is a property to rent which:

(a) has a view of the sea and
      a swimming pool   _____

(b) is near all shops   _____

(c) has a wooded garden   _____

(d) has air conditioning   _____

Check your answers on page 140.

Question 4 – Exercise 2

You and your family are on holidays in France. Read the advertisements for restaurants below and answer the questions which follow

---

La Farandole

Glaces Maison
sur place ou emporter
Salon de Thé
Bistrot Italien
12, bd des Lices

---

la Pallotte

**Cuisine de Terroir au rythme
des saisons**

Viande de Taureau
Produits de notre propre ferme
20, rue du Dr. Fanton

La Comédie

Pâtes fraîches maison
Terrasse
Fermeture hebdomadaire:dimanche et
lundi midi
10, bd G.Clémenceau

Les Saladelles

Spécialités régionales

Repas de groupe
Ouvert toute l'année
4, rue des Arènes

La Chassagnette

RESTAURANT
Potager Bio
Bibliothèque Gourmande
Réservation impératif
Le Sambuc

L'Olivier

Restaurant à thème
Buffets à volonté
Carte de vins fins
43, rue de la République

Relais de la Poste

HÔTEL – RESTAURANT
Ancien relais postal du XVIIIème siècle.
Cuisine traditionnelle
2, rue Molière

Which restaurant says it

(a) serves organic produce from the garden? _____

(b) is open all year round? _____

(c) serves home made ice-cream? _____

(d) has fresh home made pasta? _____

Check your answers on page 140.

Question 4 – Exercise 3

20h45	**Sans motif apparent.** Policier. Avec: Samuel L. Jackson. Un policier est chargé de retrouver un adolescent fugueur.

20h50	**Comme t'y es belle!** Comédie sentimentale. Avec Michèle Laroque, Aure Atika, Claire Benguigui, Géraldine Nakache. À Paris, quatre femmes de confession juive ont diversement réussi dans la vie.

20h55	**Les Disparues.** Western. Avec: Tommy Lee Jones, Cate Blanchett. Une femme se lance à la recherche de sa fille kidnappée, au Nouveau-Mexique à la fin du XIX siècle.

21h00	**La Crypte.** Fantastique. Avec: Cole Hauser, Eddie Cibrian. Un petit groupe de scientifiques découvre un terrifiant réseau de grottes sous les vestiges d'une abbaye romaine.

21h15	**Inside Man.** Policier. Avec: Clive Owen, Denzel Washington, Jodie Foster. Deux inspecteurs enquêtent sur une prise d'otages aux motivations obscures.

21h30	**Un ami parfait.** Thriller. Avec: Antoine de Caunes, Carole Bouquet. Un homme atteint d'amnésie tente avec courage de reprendre le cours de sa vie.

21h45	**L'homme sans âge.** Drame. Avec Tim Roth, Bruno Gantz. Un linguiste septuagénaire frappé par la foudre, rajeunit et se voit doté de pouvoirs étonnants.

Match the film descriptions below with the time you can see them on T.V. Check your answers on page 140.

	Film description	Time of showing
1	A man tries to rebuild his life	
2	A woman tries to find her kidnapped daughter	
3	A policeman tries to find a runaway boy	
4	Strange findings under an old abbey	

Remember...

- **Count how many ads** there are, so you will know how many you can rule out. There are usually seven ads and four answers needed.

Questions 5, 6, 7 and 8: Newspapers and magazines articles

How to deal with Questions 5, 6, 7 and 8

The next part of the Reading Section has longer pieces from French newspapers and magazines.

● Always **read the titles** and any writing that you see at the top of the text. Sometimes the answer to one of the questions may be found in the title!

● The topics in this section may be to do with accidents, local news and events.

Here are some short articles from French teenage magazines and newspapers

Question 5 – Exercise 1

Read the following article and answer the questions which follow.

PORT-VENDRES

Le maire sortant présente sa liste

Hier, Michel Strehaiano, maire sortant socialiste, a présenté sa liste en vue des prochaines élections municipales. 29 noms ont été dévoilés pour une équipe renouvelée comprenant, aux côtés de 13 membres sortants, 16 nouveaux. Une prise de contact avec les Port-Vendrais [a été établie] au cours de laquelle un bref bilan a été fait, les projets évoqués, la discussion s'est engagée, et les dates des réunions publiques ont été annoncées.

L'Indépendant, 12 février

(a) When did the Mayor announce the list of people who will take part in the next election?

_____

(b) How many new names are on the list?

_____

(c) For what events were the dates announced?

_____

Check your answers on page 140.

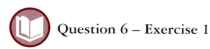

Question 6 – Exercise 1

Nageuse bizarre dans la piscine !

St. Pierre du Bois.

1. Alerté par un étrange bruit, mardi matin, Jean Rocher, a découvert qu'une vache est tombée dans la piscine municipale, qui se trouve derrière sa maison. Il a immédiatement alerté les services d'urgences et puis il est resté avec l'animal en essayant de le pacifier. Tout de suite trois équipes de pompiers sont arrivées sur place, dont l'une est spécialiste dans les captures d'animaux.

2. La vache était très stressée. Que faire ? D'abord, les pompiers ont dû vider la piscine. Puis un vétérinaire lui a fait une injection pour la calmer. Ensuite on a attaché des sangles à l'animal et peu à peu on a soulevé la vache à l'aide d'un tracteur. C'était une tâche difficile et dangereuse, à cause du poids de l'animal. Heureusement, tout s'est bien passé. Selon le vétérinaire qui l'a examinée après, la vache allait bien.

3. On cherche encore le propriétaire de la vache. En attendant, l'animal était transporté à la ferme de Monsieur Georges Duval à Belleville. Et. bonne nouvelle, elle a donné naissance mercredi à un veau, à qui on a donné le nom "Laure" – hommage à la nageuse olympique Laure Manandou !

(a) When did the incident take place? (**Part 1**)

_____

(b) Where exactly is the swimming pool? (**Part 1**)

_____

(c) Name **one** of the actions undertaken to save the animal (**Part 2**)

_____

(d) Why was the rescue dangerous? (**Part 2**)

_____

(e) What happened on Wednesday? (**Part 3**)

_____

Check your answers on page 140.

Question 7 – Exercise 1
Read the following article and answer the questions which follow.

Un bébé miraculé du tsunami va retrouver ses parents

1   Un bébé miraculé du tsunami au Sri Lanka, que neuf mères se disputaient, va retrouver ses véritables parents grâce à des tests ADN qui ont mis fin à deux mois de controverse et de passion. Un juge du tribunal de Kalmai a déclaré que les empreintes génétiques avaient établi que le couple revendiquant la parenté du 'bébé 81', garçon âgé de quatre mois, était bien ses parents biologiques.

2   Neuf mères ayant perdu des bébés dans la catastrophe du 26 décembre dans l'île revendiquaient l'enfant et la justice avait été saisie pour mettre fin à la polémique. Le bébé avait été le 81e patient admis à l'hôpital de Kalmunai, dans l'est du Sri Lanka, après le raz-de-marée [...].

3   Le bébé avait été découvert sous une pile d'ordures ayant survécu par miracle au raz-de-marée qui a fait 31 000 morts dans l'île. Il avait été sauvé par un voisin quand la mer s'était retirée.

L'Indépendant, 15 février

(a)   How many mothers are claiming that the baby is theirs? (**Part 1**)

_____

(b)   How old is the baby? (**Part 1**)

_____

(c)   What does the number 81 refer to? (**Part 2**)

_____

_____

(d)   Who saved the baby? (**Part 3**)

_____

_____

Check your answers on page 140.

Question 8 – Exercise 1
Read the following article and answer the questions which follow.

Sournia. Marie Lamole a un siècle !

1 Un évènement d'exception vient d'être célébré à la maison de retraite *Les Cèdres*. En effet, l'établissement compte désormais son troisième centenaire depuis sa création.

2 **Cent ans de vie**
Il s'agit de Marie Lamole, née le 17 janvier 1905 à Sournia, quatrième d'une famille de cinq enfants. Elle a passé sa jeunesse au village avant d'entrer dans la vie active et pendant la seconde guerre mondiale, elle a apporté une aide précieuse à sa sœur pour élever ses quatre enfants. Dans les années 60, Marie épouse Manuel Farro avec qui elle réside à Perpignan, où elle occupe un emploi de cuisinière dans une famille de négociants en vins. [...]

3 En 1965, elle prend sa retraite qu'elle passe paisiblement dans sa maison natale avant de rejoindre *Les Cèdres* en 1992. L'établissement, qui à l'origine, avait été créé pour accueillir les personnes âgées du canton héberge aujourd'hui bon nombre d'habitants de Sournia et des villages voisins.

4 **99 ans et demi d'écart...**
[...] Le directeur Claude Sire et ses collaborateurs ont souhaité réunir les résidents, les élus et les représentants de l'association autour de la centenaire et de sa famille.

À l'issue d'une journée pleine d'émotion et de bonne humeur, Marie se vit remettre les cadeaux de l'établissement du sénateur maire Paul Blanc et du conseiller général Alain Boyer, qui s'est excusé de n'avoir pu assister à cet évènement. Le plus beau cadeau pour tous étant bien sûr d'avoir pu réunir toute une famille dont le plus jeune, âgé de 6 mois, entendra sûrement parler de cette journée où entre sa tante Marie et lui-même, il y avait 99 ans et demi...

5 Longue vie à Marie, et merci à toute la famille et aux personnes ayant participé directement ou indirectement à cette journée inoubliable.

L'Indépendant, 12 février

(a) What event is being celebrated at *Les Cèdres*? (**Part 1**)

_____

(b) Who did Marie Lamole help in the Second World War? (**Part 2**)

_____

(c) Why was *Les Cèdres* built? (**Part 3**)

_____

(d) What was the best present for all concerned? (**Part 4**)

_____

(e) Who is thanked for the day? **Two** points. (**Part 5**)

_____

_____

Check your answers on page 140.

Question 9: Longer articles

How to deal with Question 9

Question 9 usually consists of an interview with a French teenager or celebrity.

- **Once again, don't forget to read the title**
- Read the text carefully as there are quite a lot of questions (8 to 10)
- **The text is divided into different parts**
- There are 8 to 10 questions on the interview.

Interviews from French magazines

 Question 9 – Exercise 1

"J'habite au pays du sourire"

Déménager à un pays 3 fois plus petit que la France, apprendre une nouvelle langue, s'adapter à une culture tout à fait différente – voilà quelques défis que Louis Lauray a dû affronter pendant les derniers deux ans. Louis (15 ans) est né à Perpignan. Son père est médecin, sa mère, sage-femme. Ils ont toujours l'envie de voyager, de faire quelque chose pour les autres humains. Donc ce n'était pas surprenant quand ils ont décidé d'aller travailler pour un organisme bénévole au Cambodge pour établir un centre medical dans un petit village. **Part 1**

Cambodge est un pays dans le sud-est de l'Asie, d'environ 14 millions d'habitants. Le voyage de la France au Cambodge est au minimum quinze heures de vol. Presque tout le monde est bouddhiste. On voit partout les moines bouddhistes, vêtus en robes oranges, qui marchent aux pieds nus sur les routes. Tout le monde les respect beaucoup. Ils pratiquent la méditation et ils ne travaillent pas, donc quand ils tendent leur bol pour demander du riz, tout le monde partage leur riz avec eux. **Part 2**

"À part le climat, la première chose qui m'a frappée, c'était la politesse des habitants. Pour se saluer, on joint les mains au niveau du visage", dit Louis. Il y a beaucoup de respect aussi pour les vieux du village. Mais les habitants sont aussi très ouverts et accueillants. Nous habitons dans une petite maison au centre du village. Beaucoup de maisons sont construites sur pilotis, car à la saison des pluies les eaux des fleuves montent et donc les chambres en haut restent bien au sec. **Part 3**

Louis et son frère Thomas sont vite assimilés dans la vie rurale. Ils vont à l'école avec les jeunes – souvent 50 élèves dans la classe. Il n'y a pas de cours l'après-midi car les élèves doivent aider les parents à nourrir les familles. Son meilleur ami cambodgien s'appelle Bunna. La vie de Bunna est très différente de celle de Louis. Son père est agriculteur et tous les jours, Bunna va aider son père dans les champs. Il coupe le riz, il va chercher du bois sec pour le four, il attrappe des crabes et des grenouilles. Leur mère en fait une soupe délicieuse ! **Part 4**

"Et qu'est-ce qu'il te manque le plus de ta vie en France, Louis ?" « Ma famille – ma soeur et mes grands-parents, car nous sommes une famille assez proche. Heureusement ma soeur est venue nous rendre visite l'année dernière. Elle m'apporté un tas de magazines français, surtout des magazines de sport. Au commencement il me manquait la télé – mes émissions favorites, comme *Koh Lanta* et *C'est pas Sorcier*. Grâce à l'Internet, je peux rester en contact avec mes copains en France. Aussi, je peux y suivre les fortunes de mon équipe de rugby favori, USAP ! » **Part 5**

(a) Apart from moving to a new country, name **one** of the challenges which Louis has faced? (**Part 1**)

_____

(b) Why did his parents want to go to Cambodia? (**Part 1**)

_____

(c) How long does it take to get from France to Cambodia? (**Part 2**)

_____

(d) Give one detail about the Buddist monks. (**Part 2**)

_____

(e) How do the Cambodians greet each other? (**Part 3**)

_____

(f) Why does school finish early? (**Part 4**)

_____

(g) Name **one** of the things Bunna does to help after school. (**Part 4**)

_____

(h) What does Louis use the Internet for? (**One** reason) (**Part 5**)

_____

Check your answers on page 141.

Question 9 – Exercise 2
Read this interview with the French actress Isild Le Besco and answer the questions which follow.

Isild Le Besco : 20 ans, ni cigale ni fourmi

1   *Dans 'Le coût de la vie', elle est une héritière honteuse. Dans la vraie vie, cette actrice, issue d'une famille nombreuse, est une généreuse sans excès.*

Chaque personnage dans 'Le coût de la vie' entretient un rapport particulier avec l'argent. Et vous ?
L'argent me rassure pour ne pas avoir à y penser. Je ne suis pas du genre à faire des folies. Ni cigale ni fourmi, mes désirs sont les mêmes que j'ai de l'argent ou pas.

2   **Vous préférez donner ou recevoir ?**
Je n'aime pas recevoir de n'importe qui. Donner est plus facile, mais c'est également une responsabilité. Donner sans distinction est aussi grave que de ne pas donner du tout.

3   **Payez-vous facilement les autres ?**
Au restaurant, j'invite ou je me fais inviter. Je déteste partager et je ne supporte pas que ceux que j'aime paient, même pour me voir au cinéma. Je préfère leur offrir une place. Mais ça me fait plaisir que les gens que je n'aime pas paient pour me voir !

4   **Votre mère, la réalisatrice Catherine Belkhodja, a élevé seule ses cinq enfants. Y avait-il des problèmes d'argent ?**
C'était difficile, mais je n'ai manqué de rien. Je me suis toujours débrouillée pour avoir ce que je voulais. J'ai fait des petits boulots très jeune. Je vendais des tee-shirts et des tuniques que je confectionnais moi-même et, à 10 ans, je faisais du baby-sitting. Nous étions trois enfants à peu près du même âge, et aucun de nous n'acceptait d'argent de poche de notre mère. On le gagnait nous-mêmes et cela nous plaisait. […]

5   **Le métier d'actrice n'est pas stable financièrement. Vous arrive-t-il de faire des choses uniquement pour l'argent ?**
Pour l'instant, je tourne régulièrement dans des films intéressants. Si cela s'arrêtait, je prendrais ce qui se présente pour vivre et cela ne me dérangerait pas. Je ne comprends pas que l'on critique un artiste qui travaille 'pour de l'argent'. Nous en sommes tous là, les artistes comme les autres. Je ne crois pas à l'art absolu.

Paris-Match n° 2828, Scoop, Interview avec Christine Haas

(*a*) What is said about her family? (**Part 1**)

_____

(*b*) What **two** things does she say about giving away money? (**Part 2**)

_____

(*c*) What does she hate when she is in a restaurant with her friends? (**Part 3**)

_____

(*d*) What does she say about people she doesn't like? (**Part 3**)

_____

(*e*) Name **two** ways Isild used to make money when she was younger. (**Part 4**)

_____

(*f*) Give **one** point she makes about pocket money. (**Part 4**)

_____

(*g*) At the moment, what is she involved in? (**Part 5**)

_____

(*h*) What does she say she doesn't understand? (**Part 5**)

_____

Check your answers on page 141.

What next?

When you have finished the Reading Comprehension section
- Check that you have attempted every question
- Make sure your answers are written clearly
- Make sure that your writing can be understood and read by the examiner
- Check that your answers are all in the right box/grid (anything written outside these will not be accepted as answers)
- Give any extra information if it is relevant

You will move to the Written Expression section of the paper when you are happy that you have answered all the questions in the Reading Comprehension section. This should have taken you about one hour. That leaves you 5 minutes to look over the paper and 45 minutes to write a letter and a postcard or a note.

Written Expression

Examination Section

	Marks Available	% of Total Marks
Written Expression	80 marks	25%

●●● Learning Objectives

1 **Set out** a letter, both informal and formal
2 **Write** a message, fax, email or postcard
3 **Learn** phrases which will help you with both these tasks
4 **Revise** the main grammar points necessary for this section of the paper
5 **Do** exercises on each grammar point

The examination step by step

- You will be asked to do **two** pieces of writing:
  1 A **letter**, formal or informal (50 marks). You will be asked to write on **four or five points**
  2 A **message**, **fax**, **email** or **postcard** (30 marks). You will be asked to write on **three points**
  3 You must write about each point to gain full marks
- The Written Expression section requires **45 minutes**: **25 minutes** for the letter, **15 minutes** for message/fax/email or postcard and **5 minutes** to look over both

On your exam paper

- Ask yourself: – '**Where** am I writing from, e.g. Paris, Dublin, Nice?'
        – '**What other words** could I use if I do not know the exact words?'
- **Jot down the tense** you need beside each point
- **Cross off** a point as you complete it
- After finishing each written question, ask yourself:
        – 'Is the **layout** in place?'
        – 'Have I covered **the correct number of points**?'
        – 'Are the **tenses** and **gender** of words correct?'

> **REVISE WISE POINTS TO NOTE**
> - **Tenses** are very important; refer to pages 91-105
> - Use your **Revision Vocabulary Lists**, on pages 147-159

What Will I Write?

What will I write in each section?

Informal letters	In this question, you will be asked to **write a letter to your friend or somebody you know well**. You will have to write on **five points** which could be in **different tenses**. The **layout** of your letter is important for marks. Make sure you attempt the **five points** as you will get some marks for each point you attempt, even if your French is not perfect.
Formal letters	In this question, you will be asked to **write to somebody you don't know well**. You will have to write about facts only (booking accommodation, looking for information for a project, etc.). The **layout** of your letter is important.
Message/Fax/ Email/Postcard	In this question, you will be asked to write a **message**, **fax**, **email** or **postcard**. You will have to **write on three points**. You are not given marks for layout but you should include it when doing this question. Attempt the **three points** as you will get marks for each point you attempt, even if your French is not perfect.
Grammar	In this book, you will find a Grammar section (pages 91-105) where the **three main tenses** you need for the Written Expression are summarised. There are **exercises** on each tense, with answers on pages 141-146. As **adjectives** and **possessive adjectives** in general are important for this section of the paper, they are also summarised with exercises (answers on page 146).

Remember…

REVISE WISE
POINTS TO NOTE

1 This is the section of the paper where **you use the French language**. If you know relevant idioms and expressions, try to include them in your writing

2 Always ask yourself **who you are writing to** (e.g. a girl or a boy)

3 Be sure you know **where you are writing the letter from**. If you are in Ireland, write an Irish town at the top of your informal letter or an Irish address at the top of a formal letter

4 Before starting a point, ask yourself: '**What tense do I need**?'

The Letters

How to deal with the letters

There are **two** types of letters:
(i)   An **informal letter** to a friend or someone your own age
(ii) A **formal letter** to somebody you do not know

Division of marks

Format/Layout	• The **layout** is important • You will get marks if you set out the letter correctly	5 marks
Effective Communication 20 marks	• You must deal with all **5 points** asked • Points must be as **clear** as possible • Marks will be awarded for **any effort** on a point	5 points x 4 marks each
Language 25 marks	• Knowledge of **tenses** is important • **Expressions** are awarded marks • Correct use of **genders** and **possessive adjectives** will be awarded marks	5 points x 5 marks each

(i) Informal letters

- You are asked to **write on five points**. Try to write four sentences for each point
- Where possible, **mention each point**, even if you have very little French. You will be rewarded for your effort
- You must use '**tu**' (*you*) to write to your penpal and '**ton, ta, tes**' (*your*)
- You must write the '**tu**' form of the verb
- You must know **present**, **past** and **future** tenses

Layout for informal letters

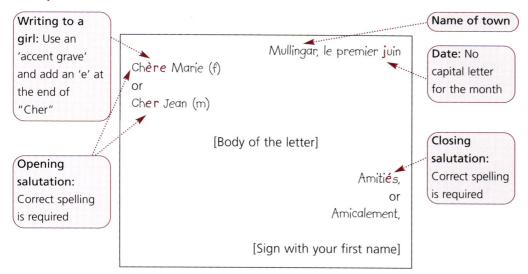

Writing to a girl: Use an 'accent grave' and add an 'e' at the end of "Cher"

Name of town

Date: No capital letter for the month

Mullingar, le premier juin

Ch**è**r**e** Marie (f)
or
Ch**e**r Jean (m)

[Body of the letter]

Opening salutation: Correct spelling is required

Amiti**é**s,
or
Amicalement,

Closing salutation: Correct spelling is required

[Sign with your first name]

Remember...

1   Words without accents lose marks. Remember the accent on the feminine form **'chère'**
2   Always use **'le'** in the date. Insert the number in front of the month
3   Watch the **first** day of the month. It is **'le premier'**
4   Do not use a capital letter for the month

Remember these points.
The correct layout earns you **5 marks** (2% of total marks for exam)

Sample informal letter (1): Junior Certificate Paper 2008

You are on a school exchange in France. You are staying with a French family and attending school. Write a letter in French to your penpal Marie-Caroline who lives in another part of France. In your letter
—   tell her about your journey from Ireland to France
—   describe the family with whom you are staying
—   say what you think of the French school
—   ask her what she will do next weekend
—   send your regards to her parents

Opening salutation – correct spelling is required

Guichen, le premier mars

Date: No capital letter for the month

Ch**è**re Marie-Caroline

Comment va tout le monde? Je suis en pleine forme. Comme tu sais je suis en France en ce moment. Je m'amuse super bien !

1st Task: Past Tense

Je suis arrivée ici il y a deux jours. J'ai pris l'avion avec quelques étudiants et profs de mon lycée. Nous avons bavardé et nous avons écouté nos ipods en avion. Le voyage n'était pas trop long. Nous sommes arrivés à Guichen à sept heures dimanche. La famille Clavel m'a rencontrée.

La famille Clavel a deux enfants et un caniche. Monsieur Clavel est drôle et est toujours de bonne humeur. Madame Clavel est très sympa et amicale. Sophie a quinze ans comme moi. Elle est gentille mais elle n'est pas sportive comme moi. Elle télécharge de la musique et aime travailler sur l'ordinateur. Sa sœur cadette s'appelle Claire. Elle a neuf ans et elle est jolie. Elle aime regarder la télévision et faire du vélo.

2nd Task: Present Tense

3rd Task: Present Tense

L'école française est bien mais la journée est très longue. Je préfère l'école en Irlande à cause de cela. Aussi, je déteste manger un grand repas à midi. L'heure de déjeuner est trop longue.

Qu'est- ce que tu feras ce week-end ? Nous ferons la grasse matinée samedi matin et ensuite nous ferons les magasins. Aussi, nous visiterons un château dimanche.

4th Task: Future Tense

5th Task: Present Tense

C'est tout pour l'instant. Je te laisse maintenant car je dois prendre mon dîner.

Dis « bonjour » à ta famille de ma part.

Écris –moi bientôt pour me donner de tes nouvelles.

Closing salutation – correct spelling is required

Amitiés,
Sheila

Phrases for informal letters

These are useful phrases for the opening, the main part and the closing of your written test.

- Try to **revise some phrases regularly** so you will know them well for the exam
- Learn the phrases **to suit the tense you are revising**, e.g. when you are revising the present tense, learn some phrases in the present tense

Opening informal letters

Je te remercie **de/pour**…	*Thank you for…*
ta lettre/ton cadeau/ta carte/le haut.	*your letter/present/card/the top.*
Je suis **en pleine forme**.	*I am in great form.*
Je suis **fatigué(e)/épuisé(e)**.	*I am tired/exhausted.*
Tout le monde va bien ici.	*Everybody is well here.*
Comment va tout le monde ?	*How is everybody?*
Désolé(e), je **n'ai pas écrit** plus tôt.	*Sorry, I have not written sooner.*
J'ai reçu ta carte il y a deux jours.	*I received your card two days ago.*

Tip

To begin the letter, remember the format/layout (look at page 67).

News about your family/friends

Mon père/mon ami gagne encore des prix au golf.	*My dad/friend is still winning prizes in golf.*
Ma sœur/ma copine est à la ferme de ma tante.	*My sister/friend is on my aunt's farm.*
Mon frère/ma copine est malade. Il/Elle a la grippe.	*My brother/friend is sick. He/she has the flu.*
Ma mère/mon ami est en vacances.	*My mother/friend is on holidays.*
Mon frère étudie à l'université.	*My brother is studying at university.*
Mon grand-père/Ma grand-mère reste chez nous pendant deux semaines.	*My grandfather/My grandmother is staying with us for two weeks.*
Nous avons un nouveau chien.	*We have a new dog.*
Nous avons une nouvelle voiture.	*We have a new car.*
Mon copain a un nouveau lapin.	*My friend has a new rabbit.*

School

Tout va bien à l'école.	*School is going well.*
J'aime toutes **les matières**.	*I like all the subjects.*
Ma **matière préférée** c'est…	*My favourite subject is…*
Mon **emploi du temps** est chargé.	*My time-table is busy.*
J'ai beaucoup de **devoirs**.	*I have a lot of homework.*
J'**étudie** beaucoup en ce moment.	*I am studying a lot at the moment.*
Je suis **épuisé(e)**.	*I am exhausted.*
Les **profs** m'énervent.	*The teachers are annoying me.*
Nous avons **un nouveau prof**.	*We have a new teacher.*
Elle/Il est sympa.	*She/He is nice.*
Il y a un nouveau **bâtiment**.	*There is a new building.*
Nous avons de nouvelles **salles de classe**.	*We have new classrooms.*
Je suis **débordé(e)** en ce moment avec mes études.	*I am overwhelmed at the moment with study.*
J'étudie **d'arrache-pied**.	*I am studying very hard.*

To do!

See also your Vocabulary Revision Lists for school and school subjects on pages 149/150.

REVISE WISE POINTS TO NOTE

Talking about exams

Les examens approchent	*The exams are near*
Nous avons **les examens blancs**	*We have the mock exams*
Je **passe** les examens	*I am sitting exams*
Je travaille/J'ai travaillé **d'arrache-pied** pour les examens	*I am working/I have worked really hard for the exams*
Je suis nerveux/nerveuse	*I am nervous*
Les examens étaient **faciles/difficiles**	*The exams were easy/difficult*
Je suis épuisé(e) après les examens	*I am exhausted after the exams*
J'espère **obtenir de bonnes notes** dans mes examens	*I am hoping to get good results in my exams*

In the past

hier	*yesterday*
la semaine dernière	*last week*
mardi dernier	*last Tuesday*
hier matin	*yesterday morning*
le week-end dernier	*last weekend*
il y a deux semaines	*two weeks ago*
il y a trois jours	*three days ago*
il y a un mois/an	*one month/a year ago*

Remember...

The **days of the week** do not begin with a capital letter in French.

The weather

Il y a/avait des nuages.

Il fait/faisait soleil.

Il fait/faisait **chaud**.	*It is/was warm.*
Il fait/faisait **froid**.	*It is/was cold.*
Il fait/faisait **beau**.	*The weather is/was nice.*
Il fait/faisait **mauvais**.	*The weather is/was bad.*
Il y a/avait du **soleil**/du **vent**.	*It is/was sunny/windy.*
Il y a/avait du **brouillard**/de la **pluie**.	*There is/was fog/rain.*
Il **pleut**/**pleuvait**.	*It rains/was raining.*

To do!

See also your Vocabulary Revision Lists, on page 158.

Activities

Present tense tous les jours, toutes les semaines, etc.	Past tense hier, la semaine dernière, le mois dernier, etc.	Future tense demain, la semaine prochaine, etc.
j'achète *I buy*	j'ai acheté *I bought*	j'achèterai *I will buy*
je nage *I swim*	j'ai nagé *I swam*	je nagerai *I will swim*
je fais du shopping *I am going shopping*	j'ai fait du shopping *I went shopping*	je ferai du shopping *I will go shopping*
je fais une promenade *I go for a walk*	j'ai fait une promenade *I went for a walk*	je ferai une promenade *I will go for a walk*
je joue au tennis/foot *I play tennis/football*	j'ai joué au tennis/foot *I played tennis/football*	je jouerai au tennis/foot *I will play tennis/football*
je m'amuse *I am enjoying myself*	je me suis amusé(e) *I enjoyed myself*	je m'amuserai *I will enjoy myself*
je loue *I rent*	j'ai loué *I rented*	je louerai *I will rent*
je passe la journée *I am spending the day*	j'ai passé la journée *I spent the day*	je passerai la journée *I will spend the day*
je rencontre *I am meeting*	j'ai rencontré *I met*	je rencontrerai *I will meet*
je vais *I am going*	je suis allé(e) *I went*	j'irai *I will go*
je visite *I am visiting*	j'ai visité *I visited*	je visiterai *I will visit*
je vois *I see*	j'ai vu *I saw*	je verrai *I will see*

Other activities

	… à l'église. (f)	… to church.
	… à la piscine.	… to the swimming pool.
	… à la plage.	… to the beach.
Je vais/suis allé(e)…	… au château.	… to the castle.
I go/went…	… au cinéma.	… to the cinema.
	… au centre commercial.	… to the shopping centre.
	… au centre-ville.	… to the city centre.
	… au musée.	… to the museum.
	… au restaurant.	… to a restaurant.
	… chez mon ami(e)/ma tante.	… to my friend's/aunt's house.
	… aux soldes.	… to the sales.
	… de l'équitation. (f)	… horse riding.
	… de la natation.	… swimming.
Je fais/J'ai fait…	… de la voile.	… sailing.
I go/went…	… du lèche-vitrine.	… window shopping.
	… un tour en ville.	… for a walk around town.
	… une promenade/balade.	… for a walk/stroll.
	… une randonnée.	… a hike.
	… des achats.	… shopping.

Reactions

C'est/C'était **chouette** !	It is/was great!	C'est/C'était **ennuyeux** !	It is/was boring!
C'est/C'était **sympa** !	It is/was nice!	C'est/C'était **affreux** !	It is/was terrible!
C'est/C'était **bon marché** !	It is/was cheap!	C'est/C'était **horrible** !	It is/was awful!
C'est/C'était **cher** !	It is/was dear!	C'est/C'était **dommage** !	It is/was a pity!
Quelle **surprise** !	What a surprise!	Quel **cauchemar** !	What a nightmare!
Quelle **journée** !	What a day!	Quelle **pitié** !	What a pity!

Describing a meal you had

Je suis allé(e) au restaurant.	I went to the restaurant.
Au petit déjeuner, il y avait	For breakfast, there were
des croissants, du pain grillé,	croissants, toast,
du jus de fruits, du café et du thé.	fruit juice, coffee and tea.
J'ai déjeuné/J'ai dîné.	I had lunch/dinner.
Comme/En entrée, j'ai pris des crudités.	For the starter I had a salad.
Comme plat principal, j'ai pris	For the main course I had
du poulet et des haricots verts.	chicken and green beans.
Comme/En dessert, j'ai pris de la glace.	For dessert, I had some ice cream.
C'était un **régal** !	It was a treat!

To do!

See your **Vocabulary Revision Lists** for food, on page 155.

REVISE WISE POINTS TO NOTE

Phrases to expand a task

In a restaurant

Les serveurs/serveuses étaient très **sympas**.	*The waiters/waitresses were very friendly.*
Il y avait une **bonne ambiance**.	*There was a good atmosphere.*
Beaucoup de Français mangeaient des moules.	*Many French people were eating mussels.*
C'était un repas français **traditionnel**.	*It was a traditional French meal.*
Le repas était **délicieux** et **pas cher**.	*The meal was delicious and cheap.*
Je me suis bien **amusé(e)**.	*I had a great time.*
Je n'ai pas aimé…	*I did not like …*

A party

Je suis allé(e) à la **soirée** de Claire/Tom.	*I went to Claire's/Tom's evening party.*
C'était son **anniversaire**.	*It was her/his birthday.*
J'ai acheté un **cadeau** pour…	*I bought a present for…*
La **fête** a commencé/fini à…	*The party began/finished at…*
La **fête** s'est terminée à…	*The party finished at…*
J'ai **rencontré**…	*I met…*
J'ai **bavardé/discuté/causé** avec…	*I chatted with…*
Quelques personnes ont **dansé**.	*Some people danced.*
J'ai aidé à **préparer**.	*I helped to prepare.*
Nous sommes allé(e)s acheter	*We went to buy food and drinks.*
de la **nourriture** et des boissons.	
Mon père est venu **me chercher** à minuit.	*My father collected me at midnight.*

An outing

J'ai **voyagé** en **car**/en **train**/en **voiture**.	*I travelled by coach/train/car.*
En route, j'ai vu…	*On the way I saw…*
Le matin, j'ai vu les **principaux monuments**.	*In the morning, I saw the main monuments.*
Nous avons **déjeuné** à une heure.	*We had our lunch at one o'clock.*
L'après-midi, nous avons fait **du tourisme**.	*In the afternoon we went sight-seeing.*
Nous sommes rentré(e)s à…	*We returned to…*
J'étais fatigué(e) mais content(e).	*I was tired but happy.*
Je suis allé(e) **nager**.	*I went for a swim.*
J'ai passé une **journée agréable**.	*I had a nice day.*
Demain, nous allons dans un **parc d'attractions**.	*Tomorrow, we are going to a theme park.*
Les toboggans étaient super.	*The slides were great.*
Le château était énorme.	*The castle was huge.*
Nous sommes rentré(e)s **sain(e)s et saufs/ves**.	*We returned home safe and well.*

Activities you will do at the weekend/next week/the future

Pour mon anniversaire	For my birthday
J'aurai une soirée	I will have a party
Je sortirai avec mes amis	I will go out with my friends
J'inviterai mes amis	I will invite my friends
Nous aurons de la musique	We will have music
Nous prendrons des frites/	We will have chips/pizza/
de la pizza/mon plat favori	my favourite dish
Mes parents m'offriront	My parents will give me
J'irai/nous irons au cinéma	I/we will go to the cinema
Je rendrai visite à	I will visit

Des cadeaux

un ipod – *An ipod*	un maillot – *a football jersey*
un portable – *A mobile phone*	de l'argent – *money*
du maquillage – *make-up*	des vêtements – *clothes*

Invitation

Est-ce que tu veux/voudrais visiter l'Irlande?	*Do you want/would you like to visit Ireland?*
Ça te dit de venir en Irlande ?	*How about coming to Ireland?*
Nous pouvons	*we can*
faire la natation/faire de la voile	*go swimming/go sailing*
visiter un musée	*go to a museum*
rencontrer mes amis	*meet my friends*
Il y a **un tas de choses** à faire ici	*there is a lot to do here*

Closing phrases for informal letters

Il **me tarde de**…	*I can't wait for…*
J'attends **avec impatience**…	*I am looking forward to…*
Écris-moi vite pour me donner de tes nouvelles.	*Write to me soon and give me your news.*
C'est tout pour l'instant.	*That's all for now.*
Je **dois te laisser**.	*I have to leave you.*
J'ai **hâte** d'avoir de tes nouvelles.	*I am looking forward to hearing your news.*
À bientôt.	*See you soon.*
J'espère **te lire** bientôt.	*I hope to hear from you soon.*
Dis « **bonjour** » à tes parents de ma part	*Tell your parents I said « hello »*
Meilleurs vœux à tes parents/ta famille	*Best wishes to your parents/family*

Remember…

- Is the **layout** correct?
- What **tense** should I use?
- Use '**faire**' for weather phrases
- **Attempt each task**

Sample informal letter (2): Junior Certificate Paper 2007

It is the month of June. You have just finished the Junior Certificate.
Write a **letter** to your French penpal Paul in which you
— thank him for his last letter.
— tell him something about the exams.
— tell him about your plans for the week-end.
— ask him if he is going to work for the summer.
— give him some news about your family.

Opening salutation – correct spelling is required

Name of town

Dublin, le 27 juin.

Date: No capital letter for the month

Cher Paul,

1st Task: Present Tense

Je te <u>remercie</u> de ta dernière lettre. J'ai reçu la lettre il y a deux semaines. Désolé, je n'ai pas écrit plus tôt. Je passais mon brevet et j'étais très occupé.

Il faisait très chaud pendant les examens. <u>J'ai étudié</u> d'arrache-pied pour l'année. <u>J'ai trouvé l'examen</u> de maths difficile mais les autres matières étaient moyennes, surtout le français. C'est ma matière préférée.

2nd Task: Past Tense

3rd Task: Future Tense

Le week-end prochain, c'est l'anniversaire de mon ami. J'attends avec impatience cet anniversaire. <u>Nous irons</u> au cinéma et après nous <u>mangerons</u> un repas à Captain Americas. Dimanche je <u>rendrai</u> visite à mes grands-parents.

4th Task: Future Tense

Est-ce que <u>tu travailleras</u> pendant l'été? Il est difficile d'obtenir un emploi en France ? L'année dernière, tu as travaillé pour ton oncle dans son restaurant. Est-ce que tu <u>retourneras</u> chez lui ? Moi, <u>j'irai</u> en vacances avec ma famille en Italie. Nous <u>louerons</u> un appartement avec une piscine.

5th Task: Present Tense

Nous <u>avons</u> un nouveau chien. Il <u>s'appelle</u> Charlie. Il <u>est</u> noir et blanc et il <u>mange</u> beaucoup. Ma soeur <u>travaille</u> à la banque pendant l'été et mon père <u>gagne</u> encore beaucoup de prix au golf. Est-ce que tu <u>joues</u> encore au golf ?

Ecris-moi vite pour me donner de tes nouvelles.

Closing salutation – correct spelling is required

Amicalement
Mark.

Remember...

● Format for the month: Use Cher for the opening salutation as you are writing to a boy: Use Amitiés/Amicalement as the closing salutation.
● Attempt the five tasks asked. Expand each point where possible.
● Knowledge of tenses is important. See pages 91-105.

REVISE WISE POINTS TO NOTE

(ii) Formal letters

- This letter is shorter than an informal letter
- **Keep to the points** you are asked to follow. In a formal letter, you can develop each point a little, but generally you make your point and move on
- Where possible, **mention each point** even if you have very little French. You will be rewarded for your effort
- You must use the '**vous**' form of the verb for '*you*' and '**votre/vos**' for '*your*'
- You must know **present**, **past** and **future** tenses

Layout for formal letters

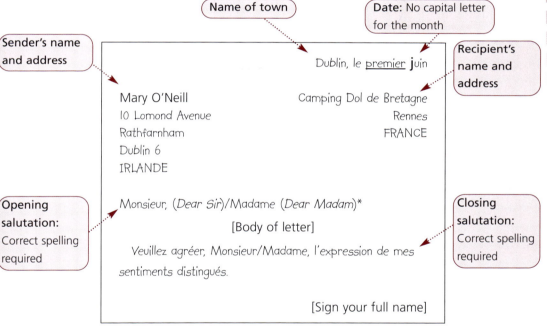

Name of town

Date: No capital letter for the month

Sender's name and address

Recipient's name and address

Opening salutation: Correct spelling required

Closing salutation: Correct spelling required

Dublin, le <u>premier</u> juin

Mary O'Neill
10 Lomond Avenue
Rathfarnham
Dublin 6
IRLANDE

Camping Dol de Bretagne
Rennes
FRANCE

Monsieur, (*Dear Sir*)/Madame (*Dear Madam*)*

[Body of letter]

Veuillez agréer, Monsieur/Madame, l'expression de mes sentiments distingués.

[Sign your full name]

* *If you are given the name of the person to whom you are writing, use that name. If not, use Monsieur/Madame.*

Remember...

1. Make sure you have sender's and recipient's **addresses** or invent an address if not given one
2. Words without **accents** lose marks
3. Always use '**le**' in the **date** and insert the **number in front of the month**. Do **not** use a **capital letter** for the month
4. Watch the first day of the month. It is '**le premier**'

Remember these points.
The correct layout earns you **5 marks** (2% of total marks for the exam).

Phrases for formal letters

Useful expressions

Je vous écris **de la part de**…	*I am writing to you on behalf of…*
Nous avons **l'intention de**…	*We intend to…*
Nous voulons **réserver du**… **au**…	*We want to book from… to…*
Je vous **serais reconnaissant(e) de** bien vouloir m'envoyer…	*I would be grateful if you would send me…*
Je **joins**…	*I enclose…*
verser une caution	*to pay a deposit*
des **installations**	*facilities*
J'espère vous lire bientôt	*I hope to hear from you soon*
par **retour de courrier**	*by return of post*
Je voudrais des renseignements sur	*I would like information about…*

Sample formal letter (1)

Write **a letter** to a tourist office requesting information for a school project on a port in France.
— ask for pictures, maps, etc.
— say you look forward to an early reply

Loughrea, le premier avril

Robert Keane
9 Hart Lane
Loughrea
Co. Galway
IRLANDE

Syndicat d'Initiative
10 Boulevard St Jean
Saint-Malo
FRANCE

Monsieur,

1st Task: Present Tense

Je <u>prépare</u> un dossier à l'école et j'ai choisi Saint-Malo. Je voudrais des renseignements sur ce port. <u>Pouvez</u>-vous m'aider ?
J'<u>ai</u> besoin de documents, d'images, de cartes et de dépliants sur l'industrie de la pêche à Saint-Malo.
J'<u>espère</u> vous lire bientôt.

2nd Task: Present Tense

Veuillez agréer, Monsieur, l'expression de mes sentiments distingués.

Robert Keane

Sample formal letter (2) – Junior Certificate Paper 2007

Your name is Martin/Martina Doyle. Your address is 4 Summerfield Drive, Patrickswell, Co. Limerick. You wish to spend some time working in a hotel in Paris during the summer holidays. Write a **formal letter** to the manager (M. or Mme Sibut, Hotel de la Paix, rue du 14 juillet, 75 000 Paris, France) in which you
— give some relevant information about yourself
— state why you wish to spend the summer working in France
— give details of your experience of hotel work
— ask for information about the hotel
(**Note**: Marks will be awarded for a formal introduction and conclusion to this letter.)

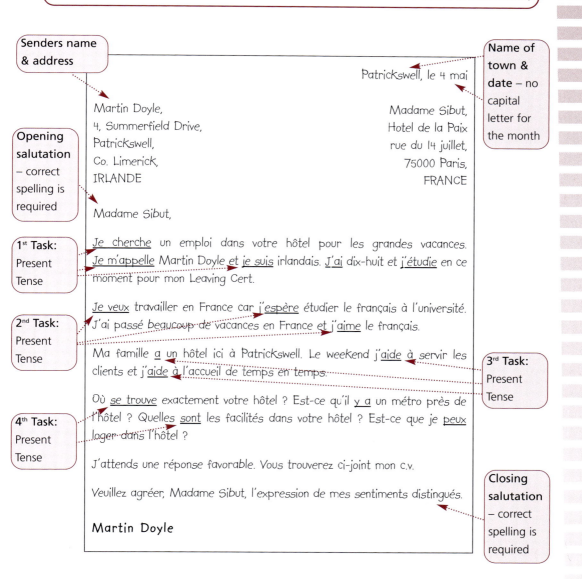

Senders name & address

Name of town & date – no capital letter for the month

Patrickswell, le 4 mai

Martin Doyle,
4, Summerfield Drive,
Patrickswell,
Co. Limerick,
IRLANDE

Madame Sibut,
Hotel de la Paix
rue du 14 juillet,
75000 Paris,
FRANCE

Opening salutation – correct spelling is required

Madame Sibut,

1st Task: Present Tense

Je cherche un emploi dans votre hôtel pour les grandes vacances. Je m'appelle Martin Doyle et je suis irlandais. J'ai dix-huit et j'étudie en ce moment pour mon Leaving Cert.

2nd Task: Present Tense

Je veux travailler en France car j'espère étudier le français à l'université. J'ai passé beaucoup de vacances en France et j'aime le français.

Ma famille a un hôtel ici à Patrickswell. Le weekend j'aide à servir les clients et j'aide à l'accueil de temps en temps.

3rd Task: Present Tense

4th Task: Present Tense

Où se trouve exactement votre hôtel ? Est-ce qu'il y a un métro près de l'hôtel ? Quelles sont les facilités dans votre hôtel ? Est-ce que je peux loger dans l'hôtel ?

J'attends une réponse favorable. Vous trouverez ci-joint mon c.v.

Veuillez agréer, Madame Sibut, l'expression de mes sentiments distingués.

Martin Doyle

Closing salutation – correct spelling is required

Messages/Faxes/Emails/Postcards

How to deal with messages/faxes/emails/postcards

- Put the **time** on a **message**
- Put the **place** and **date** on the **postcard**
- You are asked to write about **three points**. Develop each point if possible
- **If you omit a point**, you will be marked out of 20 marks, instead of 30 marks

Division of marks

Effective Communication 15 marks	• **Three points** to be mentioned • Points must be **clear** • Marks will be awarded for **any effort** at point	3 points x 5 marks each
Language 15 marks	• A knowledge of **tenses** is important • **Expressions** are awarded marks • Correct use of **genders** and **possessive adjectives** are important	3 points x 5 marks each

Messages

9 heures

Salut Marie!

Je te laisse ce petit mot pour te dire que…
I am leaving you this note to tell you that…

7 heures

Salut Luc,

Juste un petit mot pour t'informer que…
Just a note to let you know that…

14 heures

Bonjour Madame Clavel !

Juste un petit mot pour vous dire.
Just a note to tell you…

10 heures

Bonjour Monsieur Brun !

Votre ami a téléphoné pour vous dire…
Your friend telephoned to tell you…

Sample message

Leave **a message** for Aurélie, your French friend who is staying with you. Say that
— you have gone shopping for your mother who is sick
— you will be back at one o'clock
— you hope to go to the pool in the afternoon

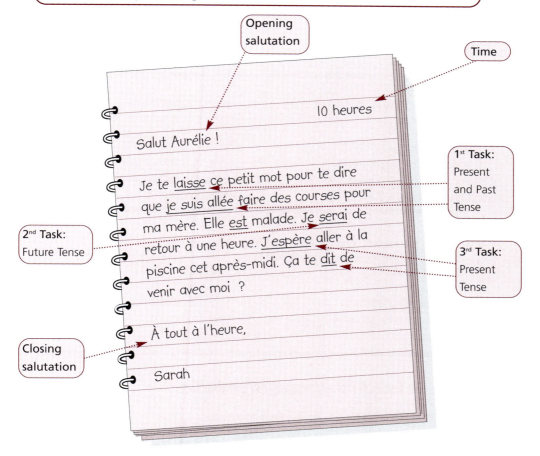

Opening salutation

Time

1st Task: Present and Past Tense

2nd Task: Future Tense

3rd Task: Present Tense

Closing salutation

> 10 heures
>
> Salut Aurélie !
>
> Je te laisse ce petit mot pour te dire que je suis allée faire des courses pour ma mère. Elle est malade. Je serai de retour à une heure. J'espère aller à la piscine cet après-midi. Ça te dit de venir avec moi ?
>
> À tout à l'heure,
>
> Sarah

Tips

REVISE WISE
POINTS TO NOTE

- Do not write 'o'clock' when writing the time. You can write '**8h**' for '*eight o'clock*'
- When you want to be respectful, when writing to an adult or when you don't know a person well: Replace '**tu**' by '**vous**', change the verb to the '**vous**' form and use '**votre/vos**' for '*your*'

Phrases for informal notes/messages/emails/faxes

Making arrangements/suggestions for messages/faxes/emails

Veux-tu **venir/aller/sortir** avec nous ?	Do you want to come/go/go out with us?
Rendez-vous à deux heures devant…	Meet at two o'clock in front of…
Téléphone-moi plus tard.	Call me later.
Je sors ce soir.	I am going out tonight.
Est-ce que tu peux… ?	Can you…?
Ça te dit de…	How about…?

Turning down arrangements for messages/faxes/emails

Désolé(e),…	Sorry,…
Je **ne peux pas** sortir.	I cannot go out.
Je **dois annuler** ma visite.	I have to cancel my visit.
Je **suis déçu(e)**.	I am disappointed.
Il ne peut pas venir.	He cannot come.

Closing phrases for informal messages/faxes/emails

À tout à l'heure.	See you later.
À plus tard.	See you later.
À demain/lundi/ce soir.	See you tomorrow/Monday/tonight.
À la semaine prochaine.	See you next week.
Je serai de retour…	I will be back…

Phrases for formal notes/messages/emails/faxes

Opening phrases

Je vous laisse ce petit mot pour vous dire que	Just a note to tell you
Katie **vous a téléphoné/vous a invité**	Katie phoned you/invited you
Juste un petit mot pour vous faire savoir que	Just a note to let you know that
Je suis allé(e) en ville en **bus**	I've gone to town on the bus
Je suis sorti(e)	I've gone out
Je **vous écris pour vous présenter mes excuses**	I am writing to you to apologise
Je n'ai pas fait mes devoirs	I didn't do my homework
Je suis rentrée tard après le match	I returned late after the match
Je **vous envoie cet e-mail** pour vous informer que	I am sending you this email to inform you that
J'arriverai lundi à dix heures	I will arrive on Monday at ten o'clock

Closing phrases for formal messages/faxes/emails

Je vous assure	I assure you
Je ne vais pas tarder	I won't delay
Je **vous promets** de rentrer pour	I promise you to return for
Je **serai de retour à**	I will return at
David **vous téléphonera**	David will phone you
J'attends votre réponse	I await your reply
Je vous prie d'accepter mes excuses	Please accept my apologies

Tips

- When writing to an adult/somebody you don't know well/ more than one person you use the **vous** form of the verb and the possessive adjectives **votre/vos**.

Sample formal message: Junior Certificate 2008 Paper

You are working as an au-pair for the Béranger family in Rennes. It is a lovely day and you have decided to take the children out. Leave a note for Mme Béranger. In your note say:
- That it is too warm in the house
- That you are gone to the park with the children
- That you will return home at half past five

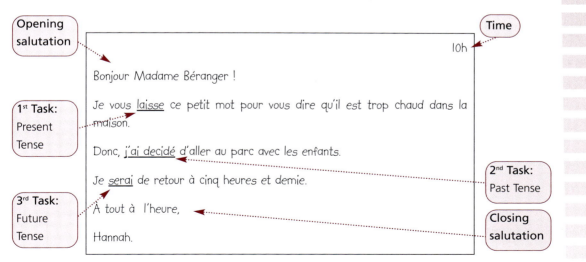

Opening salutation

Time

1st Task: Present Tense

2nd Task: Past Tense

3rd Task: Future Tense

Closing salutation

10h

Bonjour Madame Béranger !

Je vous _laisse_ ce petit mot pour vous dire qu'il est trop chaud dans la maison.

Donc, _j'ai décidé_ d'aller au parc avec les enfants.

Je _serai_ de retour à cinq heures et demie.

À tout à l'heure,

Hannah.

Faxes

Layout for faxes

À l'attention de :	To:
De :	From:
Date :	Date:

Remember…

A fax is similar to an email. Use names instead of email addresses.

Sample fax

Your French friend Alexandre is arriving next week. Send **a fax** with the following information
— you will be at the airport to meet him at 11.00 on Thursday
— would he like to go to a concert on Saturday?
— don't forget to bring swimsuit as weather is fine at the moment

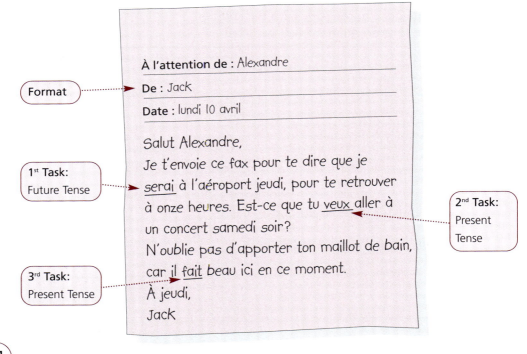

Format

À l'attention de : Alexandre

De : Jack

Date : lundi 10 avril

Salut Alexandre,
Je t'envoie ce fax pour te dire que je

1st Task: Future Tense

<u>serai</u> à l'aéroport jeudi, pour te retrouver
à onze heures. Est-ce que tu <u>veux</u> aller à

2nd Task: Present Tense

un concert samedi soir?
N'oublie pas d'apporter ton maillot de bain,

3rd Task: Present Tense

car <u>il fait</u> beau ici en ce moment.
À jeudi,
Jack

Emails

Layout for emails

De:	From:
À:	To:
Date:	Date:
Objet:	Subject:

Opening emails

Je t'envoie cet e-mail/ce courriel pour…	I am sending you this email to…
Je t'écris pour te dire/demander si…	I am writing to you to tell/ask you if…

Sample email

You are collecting your French penpal Laure from the airport. She is staying with you for two weeks. Write **an email** to her to confirm when she is arriving and where you will meet her. Say that you look forward to seeing her.

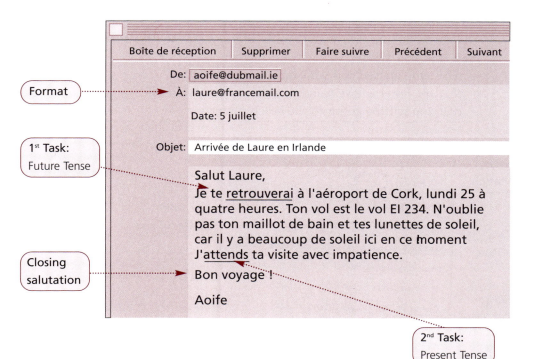

Format

1st Task: Future Tense

Closing salutation

2nd Task: Present Tense

Boîte de réception | Supprimer | Faire suivre | Précédent | Suivant

De: aoife@dubmail.ie
À: laure@francemail.com

Date: 5 juillet

Objet: Arrivée de Laure en Irlande

Salut Laure,
Je te <u>retrouverai</u> à l'aéroport de Cork, lundi 25 à quatre heures. Ton vol est le vol EI 234. N'oublie pas ton maillot de bain et tes lunettes de soleil, car il y a beaucoup de soleil ici en ce moment J'<u>attends</u> ta visite avec impatience.

Bon voyage !

Aoife

Postcards

Layout for postcards

Avignon, le 3 juin

Salut,

[Body of the postcard]

Amitiés,

Remember...

- Before you start a sentence, ask yourself: 'What **tense** do I **need**?' You must know the **present**, **past** and **future** tenses very well
- If you do not know the **exact word**, think of a different word. If you can't remember the word for 'beach' (**la plage**), use the word 'sea' (**la mer**)
- You must know '**mon, ma, mes**' and '**ton, ta, tes**'

Sample postcard (1): Junior Certificate 2006 Paper

You are on holidays with your family in Spain. Write a **postcard** to your French penpal Nicole. In your card tell her
- when you arrived and who you are with
- that the hotel is lovely and you are enjoying yourself
- that you will be going to the beach tomorrow

Opening salutation:

1st Task: Past Tense

2nd Task: Present Tense

3rd Task: Future Tense

Closing salutation:

Salou le 2 juillet

Salut Nicole,

Me voici en Espagne. Je suis arrivée ici il y a une semaine avec ma famille. L'hôtel est agréable et les facilités sont formidables.

J'irai à la plage demain car il fait du soleil ici chaque jour.

À bientôt

Sheila.

Phrases for postcards

Opening phrases for postcards

There are no marks for writing the place and the date on the postcard. However, it is better to write them as this is what people do when writing cards from holidays.

Me voici à/en…	Here I am in …
Nous voici à/en…	Here we are in …
Un grand bonjour de…	Hello from …

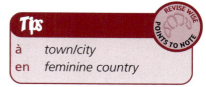

Tips

REVISE WISE
POINTS TO NOTE

à	town/city
en	feminine country

Where you are

The weather

Il fait **chaud**.	It is hot.
C'est **la canicule** !	There is a heat wave!
Il fait **beau/mauvais**.	The weather is nice/bad.
Il fait **froid**.	It is cold.
Il **neige**.	It is snowing.

To do!

REVISE WISE
POINTS TO NOTE

See your Vocabulary Revision Lists for weather, on page 158.

Describe the place

le **lieu**/l'**endroit**	*the place*
C'est **animé**.	*It is busy.*
C'est **pittoresque**.	*It is picturesque.*
C'est **agréable**.	*It is pleasant.*
La **ville** est **intéressante**.	*The town is interesting.*
Il y a beaucoup **à voir** et **à faire** ici.	*There is a lot to see and to do here.*

	… un **vieux château**.	… *an old castle.*
Il y a…	… des **magasins**.	… *shops.*
There is/are…	… une **église**.	… *a church.*
	… une **aire de jeux**.	… *a play area.*
	… une **belle plage**.	… *a beautiful beach.*

Accommodation: Where are you staying?

	… à côté d'une **ville**.	… *beside a town.*
	… à la **campagne**.	… *in the country.*
	… à l'**hôtel**.	… *in a hotel.*
	… au bord de la **mer**.	… *beside the sea.*
Je suis…	… au **centre-ville**.	… *in the middle of town.*
I am…	… dans une **famille française**.	… *with a French family.*
	… dans un **appartement**.	… *in an apartment.*
	… dans un **camping**.	… *in a campsite.*
	… dans un **gîte**.	… *in a rented holiday house.*
	… dans une **auberge de jeunesse**.	… *in a youth hostel.*
	… dans une maison.	… *in a house.*
	… près de la **plage**.	… *beside the beach.*

Who is with you?/Who are you staying with?

Je suis avec	... ma **famille**.	... *my family.*
I am with...	... mon **ami(e)**/mes **ami(e)s**.	... *my friend(s).*
	... ma **tante**/mon **oncle**.	... *my aunt, my uncle.*
Je reste chez...	... mes **grands-parents**.	... *my grand-parents.*
I am staying with...	... mon/ma **correspondant(e)**.	... *my penfriend.*

How long are you staying?

Je passe	**un mois** ici.	*I am staying here for a month.*
	un week-end	*a weekend*
	quelques jours	*a few days*
	une quinzaine de jours	*a fortnight*
	une semaine	*a week*

Closing phrases for postcards

Je te verrai bientôt.	*I will see you soon.*
À la semaine prochaine !	*See you next week!*
Je rentrerai le cinq août.	*I will be back on the fifth of August.*
À bientôt.	*See you soon.*
Dis bonjour à tout le monde de ma part.	*Say hello to everybody for me.*

To do!

See **activities you do while on holidays** pages 72 and 73.

Sample postcard (2)

You are on holiday in France with your family. Write **a postcard** to your friend Laure/Laurent and include the following
- the weather is sunny and you are enjoying yourself
- you are spending a lot of time on the beach
- send your regards to her/his parents

Remember...

REVISE WISE POINTS TO NOTE

- Is the **layout** right?
- **Attempt each task**
- What **tense** should you use?
- Use **'faire'** for weather

1st Task:
Present
Tense

2nd Task:
Present
Tense

3rd Task:
Present
Tense

Marseille, le 7 juillet

Salut Laurent !

Me voici à Marseille avec ma famille. Je m'amuse bien. Il fait soleil. Je passe beaucoup de temps à la plage. C'est super ! Je nage dans la mer tous les jours.

Je rentre en Irlande le 17 juillet. Dis 'bonjour' à tes parents de ma part.

À bientôt,
Brian

Laurent Clavel

What next?

REVISE WISE POINTS TO NOTE

When you have finished the **Written Expression section**
- **Read back** over your two pieces of writing
- Make sure your **layout is correct**
- Make sure you attempted the **five points** in the letter and the **three points** in the message, fax, email or postcard
- **Check your tenses, gender** of nouns, **possessive adjectives** and **adjectives**
- **Check your listening** and **reading comprehensions** to make sure there are no gaps
- Before you hand up your test, **make sure your number is filled** in on the outside of the test

This grammar section will help you revise what is necessary for the written section of the paper.

● There are five tenses at this level, of which **three** are necessary:
  le présent, le passé composé and **le futur**
● You will find revision tips on **adjectives** and **possessive adjectives**
● **Exercises** follow each grammar point. The **answers** are on pages 141/146.

Tenses

Le présent (Present tense)

Le présent – Regular verbs

Verbs ending in –er (1ˢᵗ group): Formation

Cross out –er: regard~~er~~. Then, add the following endings:

> **To do!**
>
> **Learn:**
>
> | je | –e | nous | –ons |
> |---|---|---|---|
> | tu | –es | vous | –ez |
> | il/elle/on | –e | ils/elles | –ent |

REVISE WISE POINTS TO NOTE

The '**je**' and '**nous**' forms of the verbs are most frequently used in the Written Expression section of the paper.

Exercise 1
Using 'passer' as a guide, complete the grid. Check your answers on page 141.

	passer to spend time	jouer to play	rester to stay	arriver to arrive
je	passe		reste	arrive
tu	passes	joues		arrives
il/elle/on	passe	joue	reste	
nous	passons		restons	arrivons
vous	passez	jouez		
ils/elles	passent	jouent		

To translate 'am/are + ing' in French, you only need the **present tense** of that verb, e.g. if you want to say:

I am arriving	j'arrive	we are spending	nous passons
I am buying	j'achète	we are staying	nous restons
I am eating	je mange	we are swimming	nous nageons

Exercise 2

Using 'louer' as a guide, complete the grid. Check your answers on page 142.

	louer to hire/to rent	**rentrer** to return/come back	**visiter** to visit	**travailler** to work
je	lou**e**	rentr**e**		travaill**e**
tu	lou**es**		visit**es**	
il/elle/on	lou**e**	rentr**e**		travaill**e**
nous	lou**ons**		visit**ons**	travaill**ons**
vous	lou**ez**	rentr**ez**	visit**ez**	
ils/elles	lou**ent**	rentr**ent**		

Exercise 3

Choose the correct verb: passe – loue – rentre – achète – joue. Check your answers on page 142.

1. Je __ une semaine au bord de la mer. (*I am spending a week by the sea.*)
2. J'__ une baguette chaque matin. (*I buy a baguette every morning.*)
3. De temps en temps, je __ un pédalo. (*From time to time, I hire a pedalo.*)
4. Je __ à la pétanque sur la plage. C'est un jeu français. (*I play bowls on the beach. It is a French game.*)
5. Je __ en Irlande lundi. (*I am returning to Ireland on Monday.*)

Were you right?

1. '**Passer**' means *to spend*. '**e**' is the ending of the '**je**' form of the present tense. The answer is '**passe**'.
2. '**j**'' means the verb must begin with a **vowel** (**e, i, o** or **u**). The answer is '**achète**'.
3. '**Louer**' means *to hire*. '**e**' is the ending of the '**je**' form of the present tense. The answer is '**loue**'.
4. '**Jouer**' means *to play*. '**e**' is the ending of the '**je**' form of the present tense. The answer is '**joue**'.
5. '**Rentrer**' means *to return, to go back*. '**e**' is the ending of the '**je**' form of the present tense. The answer is '**rentre**'.

Verbs spelt differently in the 'nous' form

Verbs ending in **–ger** keep the **'e'** before vowels **'a'** and **'o'** as in nager (*to swim*), manger (*to eat*), plonger (*to dive*), changer (*to change*).

Exercise 4
Using 'nager' as a guide, complete the grid. Check your answers on page 142.

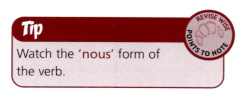

Tip

Watch the **'nous'** form of the verb.

REVISE WISE
POINTS TO NOTE

	nager to swim	**manger** to eat	**plonger** to dive	**voyager** to travel
je	nag**e**		plong**e**	voyag**e**
tu	nag**es**	mang**es**		voyag**es**
il/elle/on	nag**e**	mang**e**	plong**e**	
nous	nag**eons**			
vous	nag**ez**	mang**ez**		
ils/elles	nag**ent**	mang**ent**		

Exercise 5
Write the correct form of the verb and translate into English. Check your answers on page 142.

1   Nous (loger) dans un hôtel.
2   Nous (nager) dans la piscine.
3   Nous (manger) dans le Café de Soleil
4   Nous (plonger) dans la mer.
5   Nous (voyager) en avion à Paris.

Reflexive verbs

Reflexive verbs ending in –er (*some of them associated with holidays*)

Reflexive verbs are verbs which use **two pronouns**, e.g. I (*myself*), they (*themselves*), '**je me** lave' (*I wash myself*), '**elle s**'habille' (*she dresses herself*).

Exercise 6

Using 's'amuser' as a guide, complete the grid. Check your answers on page 143.

	s'amuser *to enjoy oneself*	se reposer *to relax*	se lever *to get up*	se promener *to go for a walk*
je	m'amuse	me repose		
tu	t'amuses		te lèves	
il/elle/on	s'amuse	se repose		se promène
nous	nous amusons			
vous	vous amusez	vous reposez	vous levez	
ils/elles	s'amusent			se promènent

Tip

REVISE WISE
POINTS TO NOTE

Treat these verbs as any other –er
verb in the **present tense**.

Exercise 7

Write the correct form of the verb and translate into English. Check your answers on page 143.

1   Je (m'amuser) à Saint-Malo.
2   Le matin, je (se reposer).
3   L'après-midi, je (se promener) avec ma sœur et mon frère.
4   Nous (se baigner) dans la mer.
5   Je (se coucher) tard tous les soirs.

Exercise 8

Translate the following sentences into French. Check your answers on page 143.

1   I get up late every morning.
2   I am staying here for two weeks.
3   Sometimes, I hire a boat.
4   We visit the museums in the area.
5   We are enjoying ourselves here.

Le présent – Irregular verbs

Here is a group of verbs which **do not follow rules** and **are essential** for the Written Expression section of the paper.

To do!

Learn these verbs by heart.

Examples

	aller *to go*	**avoir** *to have*	**boire** *to drink*	**devoir** *to have to/must*
je/j'	vais	ai	bois	dois
tu	vas	as	bois	dois
il/elle/on	va	a	boit	doit
nous	allons	avons	buvons	devons
vous	allez	avez	buvez	devez
ils/elles	vont	ont	boivent	doivent

	écrire *to write*	**être** *to be*	**faire** *to do/to make*	**sortir** *to go out*
je/j'	écris	suis	fais	sors
tu	écris	es	fais	sors
il/elle/on	écrit	est	fait	sort
nous	écrivons	sommes	faisons	sortons
vous	écrivez	êtes	faites	sortez
ils/elles	écrivent	sont	font	sortent

	pouvoir *to be able*	**prendre** *to take*	**venir** *to come*	**vouloir** *to wish/to want*
je	peux	prends	viens	veux
tu	peux	prends	viens	veux
il/elle/on	peut	prend	vient	veut
nous	pouvons	prenons	venons	voulons
vous	pouvez	prenez	venez	voulez
ils/elles	peuvent	prennent	viennent	veulent

To do!

See also your **Verb Table**, on pages 160-163.

Exercise 9

Write the correct form of the verb. Use the grids on page 94 to do this exercise. Check your answers on page 143.

1   Nous (faire) de la natation tous les jours. *(We go swimming every day.)*
2   Le soir, je (aller) à la salle de jeux du camping. *(In the evening I go to the games room of the campsite.)*
3   Nous (être) dans un camping au bord de la mer. *(We are in a campsite beside the sea.)*
4   Je (vouloir) une glace. *(I want an ice cream.)*
5   Nous (prendre) le car pour voyager. *(We take the coach to travel.)*

Exercise 10

Write the correct form of the verb and translate into English. Check your answers on page 143.

1   Je (boire) un café au lait chaque matin.
2   Nous (aller) à la piscine chaque après-midi.
3   Il (faire) beau en ce moment.
4   Je (sortir) avec mes amis le week-end.
5   Nous (vouloir) visiter un château pendant nos vacances.

Exercise 11

Translate the following sentences into French. Check your answers on page 143.

1   We drink a lot of water.
2   We go sailing every day.
3   We can see the beach from our window.
4   It is sunny.
5   I have to go out now.

Le présent – Verbs ending in –ir (2ⁿᵈ group)

The following group of verbs is not often used in the Written Expression section of the paper. However, **you should know the endings.**

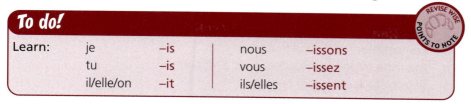

To do!					
Learn:	je	–is	nous	–issons
	tu	–is	vous	–issez
	il/elle/on	–it	ils/elles	–issent

Examples

	finir	**choisir**
	to finish	*to choose*
je	fin**is**	chois**is**
tu	fin**is**	chois**is**
il/elle/on	fin**it**	chois**it**
nous	fin**issons**	chois**issons**
vous	fin**issez**	chois**issez**
ils/elles	fin**issent**	chois**issent**

Le présent – Verbs ending in –re (3ʳᵈ group)

The following group of verbs is not often used in the Written Expression section of the paper. However, you should **know the endings.**

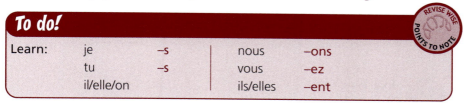

To do!					
Learn:	je	–s	nous	–ons
	tu	–s	vous	–ez
	il/elle/on		ils/elles	–ent

Examples

	attendre	**répondre**
	to wait for	*to reply*
je/j'	attend**s**	répond**s**
tu	attend**s**	répond**s**
il/elle/on	attend	répond
nous	attend**ons**	répond**ons**
vous	attend**ez**	répond**ez**
ils/elles	attend**ent**	répond**ent**

Exercise 12

Write the correct form of the verb and translate into English. Check your answers on page 144.

1. J'(attendre) ta lettre avec impatience.
2. Nous t'(attendre) devant le supermarché.
3. Les vacances (finir) dans trois jours.
4. Ma tante (répondre) régulièrement à mes lettres.
5. Je (choisir) le restaurant ce soir.

Le présent in action

Exercise 13

Here is an opening paragraph of a letter. *Underline the present tense. There are nine examples.* Check your answers on page 144.

> Dublin, le 2 juillet
>
> Chère Cloé,
>
> Comment vas-tu ? Je suis en pleine forme. Toute la famille va bien. En ce moment, je cherche des livres pour le lycée. Je range ma chambre aussi. Mon père achète une nouvelle voiture. Elle est verte. Mon frère a un nouveau chien. Il s'appelle Chippie.
>
> Amitiés,
> Mary

Exercise 14

Here is a brief postcard in the present tense. *Underline the present tense. There are six examples.* Check your answers on page 144.

> Paris, le 3 juin
> Salut Pascale,
>
> Je passe une semaine à Paris avec ma famille. Il fait vraiment très beau. Je fais des achats tous les jours. Je m'amuse beaucoup et je visite de très grands musées. Je rentre en Irlande le 17 juillet.
>
> Au revoir,
> Siobhán

Pascale Leblanc

Le passé composé (Past tense)

You need this tense to write about any completed action in the past, e.g. *I went, I spoke.*

Le passé composé – Formation

The passé composé tense is made of **two parts**:

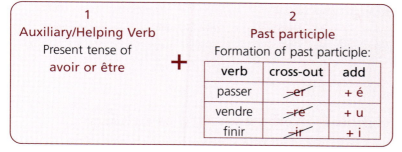

	1 Auxiliary/Helping Verb Present tense of **avoir or être**	**+**	2 Past participle Formation of past participle:		

verb	cross-out	add
passer	~~er~~	+ é
vendre	~~re~~	+ u
finir	~~ir~~	+ i

j'ai	+	mangé
j'ai	+	parlé
j'ai	+	joué
j'ai	+	regardé
je suis	+	passé
j'ai	+	fini
j'ai	+	vendu

Le passé composé – Verbs with 'avoir' as auxiliary

Example of a verb that uses 'avoir' to make the past tense (passé composé):

passer			
j'	ai	passé	*I spent*
tu	as	passé	*you spent*
il/elle/on	a	passé	*he/she spent*
nous	avons	passé	*we spent*
vous	avez	passé	*you spent*
ils/elles	ont	passé	*they spent*

Tips

- When using the passé composé, always ask yourself: 'Have I an **auxiliary verb** and a **past participle**?'
- In general, the spelling of the **past participle does not change when 'avoir'** is used

REVISE WISE
POINTS TO NOTE

Other examples

j'**ai** acheté	*I bought*	nous **avons** acheté	*we bought*
j'**ai** loué	*I hired*	nous **avons** loué	*we hired*
j'**ai** visité	*I visited*	nous **avons** visité	*we visited*
j'**ai** fini	*I finished*	nous **avons** fini	*we finished*
j'**ai** vendu	*I sold*	nous **avons** vendu	*we sold*

Le passé composé – Irregular verbs

The following useful verbs have **irregular past participles**:

avoir (*to have*)	→	**eu**	lire (*to read*) → **lu**
boire (*to drink*)	→	**bu**	mettre (*to put*) → **mis**
conduire (*to drive*)	→	**conduit**	pouvoir (*to be able*) → **pu**
devoir (*to have to*)	→	**dû**	prendre (*to take*) → **pris**
écrire (*to write*)	→	**écrit**	recevoir (*to receive*) → **reçu**
être (*to be*)	→	**été**	voir (*to see*) → **vu**
faire (*to do/to make*)	→	**fait**	vouloir (*to want*) → **voulu**

Le passé composé – Verbs with 'être' as auxiliary

The following **13 verbs** and **all reflexive verbs** use the verb '**être**' to make the **passé composé**.

Verbs Using Auxiliary 'être'

aller	*to go*
arriver	*to arrive*
descendre	*to get/come down*
entrer	*to enter/go in*
monter	*to go up*
mourir	*to die*
naître	*to be born*
partir	*to leave/depart*
retourner	*to come back/return*
rester	*to stay/remain*
sortir	*to go out*
tomber	*to fall*
venir	*to come*

Useful Reflexive Verbs

s'approcher	*to approach/come close*
s'amuser	*to enjoy yourself*
se baigner	*to bathe, to swim*
se blesser	*to injure yourself*
se coucher	*to go to bed*
se couper	*to cut oneself*
s'habiller	*to get dressed*
se laver	*to wash (one's hands, face)*
se lever	*to get up*
se relaxer	*to relax*
se reposer	*to rest*
se réveiller	*to wake up*
se promener	*to go for a walk*
se faire bronzer	*to sunbathe*

Tip

The past participle of the verbs using 'être' as auxiliary **has to agree with** the person or thing doing the action.

aller *to go*	gender	s'amuser *to have fun*
je suis allé		je me suis amusé
je suis allée		je me suis amusée
tu es allé		tu t'es amusé
tu es allée		tu t'es amusée
il est allé		il s'est amusé
elle est allée		elle s'est amusée
nous sommes allés		nous nous sommes amusés
nous sommes allés		nous nous sommes amusés
nous sommes allées		nous nous sommes amusées
vous êtes allés		vous vous êtes amusés
vous êtes allés		vous vous êtes amusés
vous êtes allées		vous vous êtes amusées
ils sont allés		ils se sont amusés
ils sont allés		ils se sont amusés
elles sont allées		elles se sont amusées

Le passé composé – Verbs with 'être' as auxiliary – Formation

The past participle of most of the verbs using 'être' as their auxiliary is formed in the same way as the past participle of verbs using 'avoir' as their auxiliary:

verbs ending in	past participle
–er ————————➤	é
–ir ————————➤	i
–re ————————➤	u

The following are irregular past participles:

verbs	past participle
naître ————————➤	né
mourir ————————➤	mort
venir ————————➤	venu

Exercise 15
In this opening letter, try to find six verbs in the passé composé.
Check your answers on page 144.

Galway, le 2 juillet

Chère Élodie,

Comment vas-tu ? Moi, ça va bien. J'ai passé une semaine à Paris avec ma famille. Il a fait très beau toute la semaine. Nous sommes restés dans un hôtel et j'ai fait de la natation tous les jours, car il y avait une piscine à côté de l'hôtel. J'ai fait des achats de temps en temps. Je me suis bien amusée.

Amitiés,
Siobhán

Remember...

REVISE WISE
POINTS TO NOTE

Verb with 'avoir':
- 'Have I an auxiliary/helping verb and a past participle?'
- 'Have I the correct auxiliary/helping verb?'

Verb with 'être':
- 'Who is doing the action?'
- 'Have I made the past participle agree with the subject?'
- Agreement means adding 'e', 's' or 'es' to the past participle

Who is doing the action?

QUENTIN EST ARRIVÉ

LOLA EST ARRIVÉE

SINÉAD ET AOIFE SONT ARRIVÉES

HUGO ET BAPTISTE SONT ARRIVÉS

HANNAH ET LUC SONT ARRIVÉS À GALWAY

Le futur (Future tense)

The future tense is used when you want to write about what you are going to do **tomorrow** or the **following week** and about what **you will** do later.

Le futur – Formation

Leave the –er and –ir verbs in the **infinitive form** and then **add the following endings**:

To do!

Learn:					
	je	–ai	nous	–ons	
	tu	–as	vous	–ez	
	il/elle/on	–a	ils/elles	–ont	

Drop the 'e' in –re verbs and add the same endings.

Le futur – Important verbs for letters

Exercise 16

Complete the grid, using 'passer' as your guide. Check your answers on page 144.

	passer to spend	**jouer** to play	**rester** to stay	**arriver** to arrive
je	passer**ai**	jouer**ai**	rester**ai**	
tu	passer**as**		rester**as**	arriver**as**
il/elle/on	passer**a**	jouer**a**		
nous	passer**ons**			arriver**ons**
vous	passer**ez**	jouer**ez**	rester**ez**	
ils/elles	passer**ont**	jouer**ont**		arriver**ont**

Exercise 17

Complete the grid, using 'louer' as your guide. Check your answers on page 145.

	louer to hire/to rent	**retourner** to return	**visiter** to visit	**regarder** to look at/watch
je	louer**ai**		visiter**ai**	regarder**ai**
tu	louer**as**	retourner**as**		
il/elle/on	louer**a**	retourner**a**	visiter**a**	
nous	louer**ons**		visiter**ons**	
vous	louer**ez**	retourner**ez**		regarder**ez**
ils/elles	louer**ont**	retourner**ont**	visiter**ont**	regarder**ont**

Tips

- Remember the **endings of the future tense**
- Watch the **–re** verbs. Remember to drop the '**e**' before you add the endings
- In the **present tense**, the 'they' form ends in '**ent**'. However, in the **future tense** the 'they' form ends in '**ont**'

Le futur –ir verbs

Exercise 18

Complete the grid, using 'finir' as your guide. Check your answers on page 145.

	finir to finish	**partir** to leave	**sortir** to go out	**choisir** to choose
je	finir**ai**		sortir**ai**	choisir**ai**
tu	finir**as**	partir**as**	sortir**as**	
il/elle/on	finir**a**	partir**a**		choisir**a**
nous	finir**ons**	partir**ons**	sortir**ons**	
vous	finir**ez**		sortir**ez**	choisir**ez**
ils/elles	finir**ont**	partir**ont**		choisir**ont**

Exercise 19

Link the subject to the verb and translate the sentences into English. Check your answers on page 145.

1 Nous…	(a) … choisirai un restaurant pour le repas.
2 Tu…	(b) … resterons ici pendant deux semaines.
3 Ma famille et moi…	(c) … visiteras un château lundi prochain.
4 Ma sœur…	(d) … retournerons en Irlande la semaine prochaine.
5 Je…	(e) … finira ses devoirs demain.

Were you right?

1 '**Nous**' needs '**ons**' in the future tense. The answer is either '**resterons**' or '**retournerons**'.

2 '**Tu**' needs '**as**' in the future tense. The answer is '**visiteras**'.

3 '**Ma famille et moi**' requires the '**nous**' form of the verb, therefore, '**ons**' is the ending that is needed. The answer is '**resterons**' or '**retournerons**'.

4 '**Ma soeur**' needs '**a**' in the future tense. The answer is '**finira**'.

5 '**Je**' needs '**ai**' in the future tense. The answer is '**choisirai**'.

Le futur –re verbs drop the 'e'

Examples

	attendre to wait for	*perdre* to lose
je/j'	attendr**ai**	perdr**ai**
tu	attendr**as**	perdr**as**
il/elle/on	attendr**a**	perdr**a**
nous	attendr**ons**	perdr**ons**
vous	attendr**ez**	perdr**ez**
ils/elles	attendr**ont**	perdr**ont**

To do!
REVISE WISE POINTS TO NOTE

Learn the following verbs associated with **holidays**:

j'achèter**ai**	*I will buy*
je m'amuser**ai**	*I will enjoy myself*
je manger**ai**	*I will eat*
je nager**ai**	*I will swim*
je me promèner**ai**	*I will go for a walk*
je rentrer**ai**	*I will be back home*
je me reposer**ai**	*I will relax*
je visiter**ai**	*I will visit*
je voyager**ai**	*I will travel*

Remember...
REVISE WISE POINTS TO NOTE

The **endings** for all verbs in the **future tense** are the same.

Le futur – Some examples of irregular verbs

	avoir to have	*aller* to go	*etrê* to be	*faire* to do/to make
je/j'	aur**ai**	ir**ai**	ser**ai**	fer**ai**
tu	aur**as**	ir**as**	ser**as**	fer**as**
il/elle/on	aur**a**	ir**a**	ser**a**	fer**a**
nous	aur**ons**	ir**ons**	ser**ons**	fer**ons**
vous	aur**ez**	ir**ez**	ser**ez**	fer**ez**
ils/elles	aur**ont**	ir**ont**	ser**ont**	fer**ont**

To do!
REVISE WISE POINTS TO NOTE

See your **Verb Table**, on pages 160-163, for further examples of **irregular verbs in the future**.

Exercise 20
Change the verbs in brackets into the future tense and translate them into English. Check your answers on page 145.

1. Je (être) de retour à huit heures.
2. Nous (faire) une excursion demain.
3. Elle (aller) au marché samedi.
4. Ils (avoir) des vacances en juillet.
5. Je te (voir) plus tard.
6. Nous (pouvoir) faire du shopping ensemble.
7. Est-ce que tu (venir) nous voir bientôt ?
8. Pierre et Luc, vous (devoir) être au café à neuf heures.

Les Adjectifs Possessifs (Possessive adjectives)

The possessive adjectives (my, your, his/her, our, their) are important for the Written Expression section, as you will be saying 'my hotel', 'my family', 'our apartment', etc.

- To decide which possessive adjective to use, look at the noun it describes
- Ask yourself: Is the word coming after the possessive adjective masculine/feminine/a vowel/plural?

Les adjectifs possessifs – Formation

	masculine singular	all singular vowels*	feminine singular	all plural nouns
my	mon	mon	ma	mes
your	ton	ton	ta	tes
his	son	son	sa	ses
her	son	son	sa	ses
our	notre	notre	notre	nos
your	votre	votre	votre	vos
their	leur	leur	leur	leurs

*A lot of French nouns which start with an 'h', are treated as vowels, e.g. hôpital, hôtel.

Examples				
mes parents	my parents	mon ami (m)	my friend
mes vacances	my holidays	mon amie (f)	my friend
nos vacances	our holidays	notre hôtel	our hotel
mon appartement	my apartment	leur hôtel	their hotel

Exercise 21

*Write the correct possessive adjective (**my**, **your** or **our**) in front of the following words, and translate the sentences into English.* Check your answers on page 146.

1 __ hôtel est au bord de la mer.
2 __ camping est grand.
3 Je rencontre __ amis chaque jour.
4 Je reste dans un gîte avec __ famille pour deux semaines.
5 __ prof organise un voyage scolaire à Londres.
6 Comment se passent __ vacances ?
7 __ père va bien.
8 __ amis s'amusent beaucoup ici.
9 Comment vont __ parents ?
10 __ vol est le deux juillet à trois heures.

Tips

- Ask yourself: What is the gender of the word coming after the possessive adjective?
- 'My' and 'our' are the most commonly used possessive adjectives for the Written Expression section

REVISE WISE
POINTS TO NOTE

Les Adjectifs – Feminine and Plural Forms

- If the noun/word you wish to describe is feminine, the adjective must be feminine
- If the noun/word you wish to describe is plural the adjective must be plural
- If the noun/word you wish to describe is feminine plural the adjective must be feminine plural
- The masculine form is the form you find in the dictionary list

Les adjectifs – Feminine and plural forms

Most adjectives

	masculine	feminine add 'e'	masculine plural add 's'	feminine plural add 'es'
blue	bleu	bleue	bleus	bleues
big/tall	grand	grande	grands	grandes
small/short	petit	petite	petits	petites

Tips

- If an adjective ends in an 'e', you do not add an 'e' to make it feminine, e.g. rouge (m), rouge (f)
- If an adjective ends in 's', you do not add an 's' to make it plural, e.g. gris (m, s), gris (m, pl)

REVISE WISE POINTS TO NOTE

Adjectives ending in 'eux' in masculine

	masculine	feminine becomes 'euse'	masculine plural no change	feminine plural becomes 'euses'
dangerous	dangereux	dangereuse	dangereux	dangereuses
happy	heureux	heureuse	heureux	heureuses
lazy	paresseux	paresseuse	paresseux	paresseuses
serious	sérieux	sérieuse	sérieux	sérieuses

Adjectives ending in 'er' in masculine

	masculine	feminine becomes 'ère'	masculine plural add 's'	feminine plural becomes 'ères'
dear	cher	chère	chers	chères
first	premier	première	premiers	premières
last	dernier	dernière	derniers	dernières

Adjectives ending in 'if' in masculine

	masculine	feminine becomes 'ive'	masculine plural add 's'	feminine plural becomes 'ives'
active	actif	active	actifs	actives
agressive	agressif	agressive	agressifs	agressives
creative	créatif	créative	créatifs	créatives
sporty	sportif	sportive	sportifs	sportives

Adjectives ending in 'en' or 'on' in masculine

	masculine	feminine add 'n' and 'e'	masculine plural add 's'	feminine plural add 'n' and 'es'
average	moyen	moyenne	moyens	moyennes
cute	mignon	mignonne	mignons	mignonnes
good	bon	bonne	bons	bonnes
Italian	italien	italienne	italiens	italiennes
old/former	ancien	ancienne	anciens	anciennes

Irregular adjectives

The following irregular adjectives must be learned.

	masculine	feminine	masculine plural	feminine plural
beautiful	beau/bel*	belle	beaux	belles
dry	sec	sèche	secs	sèches
fresh	frais	fraîche	frais	fraîches
nice	gentil	gentille	gentils	gentilles
long	long	longue	longs	longues
new	nouveau/nouvel*	nouvelle	nouveaux	nouvelles
old	vieux/vieil*	vieille	vieux	vieilles
red (hair)	roux	rousse	roux	rousses
white	blanc	blanche	blancs	blanches

* 'Beau' becomes 'bel', 'nouveau' becomes 'nouvel' and 'vieux' becomes 'vieil' when they are placed
before a noun in the singular beginning with a vowel or an 'h'.

The following adjectives go before the noun

Most adjectives go after the noun they describe, but the following list always go **before** the noun.

beau	*beautiful*	long	*long*
bon	*good*	mauvais	*bad*
grand	*big*	nouveau	*new*
jeune	*young*	petit	*small*
joli	*pretty*	vieux	*old*

Exercise 22

Fill in the grid with the correct form of the adjective. Check your answers on page 146.

	masculine	feminine	masculine plural	feminine plural
boring	ennuy**eux**		ennuy**eux**	
old		vie**ille**		
nice			genti**ls**	
small	peti**t**		peti**ts**	
serious	séri**eux**			
aggressive				agress**ive**

Exercise 23

Write the correct form of the adjective and translate into English. Check your answers on page 146.

1 La maison est (bleu) et (noir).
2 La fille est (grand) et (joli).
3 Les chaises sont (petit) et (noir).
4 Marie est (heureux) au lycée.
5 La semaine (dernier), je suis allé(e) à Wexford.
6 Le mois (dernier), il a visité l'Irlande.
7 Michelle est (sportif) et (mignon).
8 « Je suis (moyen) en maths et je suis (fort) en français », dit Claire.
9 J'ai passé une (long) journée au lycée.
10 Ma grand-mère est (vieux).

Section 1: Listening Comprehension

Section A

- The format of the first question on the 2009 paper is one with which you should be familiar. You have to identify the **subject matter** of **three** conversations
- There are **five possible answers**
- Each conversation is played **twice**

> **Tip**
> Look back to pages 4-10.

> Your examination will start with **three** conversations. In the case of each conversation say whether it is about
> (a) buying clothes;
> (b) getting something to eat;
> (c) someone feeling unwell;
> (d) making plans for the weekend **or**
> (e) a new teacher at school.

How do you find the answer?

First Conversation

The boy starts by saying "j'ai faim" – *I'm hungry*, "je peux avoir un goûter ?" – *may I have a snack?* This should give you a good clue that this conversation is to do with eating **(b)**. His mother offers him "fruit", but he asks for "chocolat"; his mother also says "les pommes sont délicieuses" – *the apples are delicious*, all items of food, so from these hints you can be sure the answer is conversation **(b)**.

Second Conversation

The boy mentions "un nouveau prof de géo" – *a new geography teacher*. If you miss this, someone is referred to as being "stricte" and "sévère" and there is a reference to "ma matière préférée" – *my favourite subject*, which tells you that the conversation has something to do with school. The word "la géo" is also mentioned twice. The correct answer is, therefore, **(e)**.

Third Conversation

The man says "je ne me sens pas bien" – *I don't feel well* and also says "j'ai pris un coup de soleil" – *I took too much sun/I've got sunstroke*. To help you further he asks for "aspirine". At the end of the conversations the woman says "vous serez bientôt mieux" – *you'll be better soon*. The answer to this conversation is **(c)**.

Section B

- This section is similar in format to what has been asked in previous years
- **Two people**, one female and one male, speak about themselves
- You are asked for **personal details** about each person
- Each conversation is played for you **three times**, with a pause between each playing for you to write down the information

How do you find the answer?

First speaker: Élodie

Speaker	What you hear	What you should write down
Name	Élodie	Élodie
Nationality	**canadienne**, also mentions Montréal and Québec	Canadian
Birthday	sept avril	7th April
Mother's job	ma mère travaille comme **infirmière**	Nurse
Colour of eyes	les yeux **gris**	grey
Two musical instruments played	je joue du **violon** et du **piano**	violin and piano
One school subject she likes	je préfère les **matières scientifiques**, la **biologie**, la **chimie**	science subjects/biology or chemistry
Reason for her choice of career	j'aime beaucoup **aider les autres**	likes to help people/others

Tip

The voice of this speaker indicates it's an adult who is speaking. Also the questions show he has children and a wife, so remember this when answering the question on his age.

REVISE WISE POINTS TO NOTE

Second speaker: Charles

Speaker	What you hear	What you should write down
Name	Charles	Charles
Age	quarante-cinq	45
Number of children	nos "**trois** enfants"	3
Job	je travaille à la SNCF je conduis les trains le nouveau TGV Strasbourg – Paris	Driver for SNCF or Train driver or Drives the TGV

Two details he gives about Strasbourg	une ville **historique**
	que les **touristes aiment beaucoup**
	ses **vieilles maisons**
	sa belle **cathédrale**
	ses petites **rues étroites**
		Any **two** of the following
		  an historic city
		tourists like it/like it a lot
		  old houses/buildings
		  beautiful cathedral
		  little narrow streets

Two things he likes to do in the country	je fais du **vélo**
	je joue aux **boules**
	je **nage** dans la **rivière**
		Any **two** of the following
		  cycles
		  plays bowls
		  swims (in the river)

Why his wife wants to stay in Strasbourg	car elle **aime son travail** (comme secrétaire dans une banque)	she likes her job/work (as a secretary in a bank)

Section C

There is no change in the format of this section in 2009
- You are asked to listen to **five separate conversations**, each with a different topic or theme
- There are **two questions** to be answered on each conversation
- Each of these conversations is played **twice**

First Conversation

> 1   (a)   Where does the tourist wish to go?
>   What directions does the man give her?

How do you find the answer?

(a)   The woman asks "où se trouve **le château**", *the castle*. The man repeats "le château", which should help you.

(b)   The man says "allez **tout droit**" – *go straight ahead* and "prenez la **deuxième rue à gauche**" – *take the second turn to the left*. The woman repeats these instructions, so you will, in fact, hear the instructions four times.

Tip
Revise your street directions
– see page 24.

Second Conversation

> 2   (a)   For which day of the week does the woman book concert tickets?
>   (b)   Spell the woman's surname. Write one letter in each box

How do you find the answer?

(a)   You must know your days of the week! There is no clue here to help you – the woman says "**lundi** prochain" – *Monday next*

(b)   There are six letters to be filled in. Don't try to get the spelling in one go! The woman spells her name, then the man repeats the spelling. So, you will hear this twice on each playing (four times in all). Listen to the sound of the name, that might help you also. She says "T (tay), R (er), U (ooh), O (oh), N (en), G (jay) this last letter is tricky". Remember how the French pronounce the letter G! Her name is *T R O U N G* – not a very common French surname!

Third Conversation

> 3   **(a)**   For which event is the boy buying flowers?
>
>   **(b)**   How much does he pay for them?

How do you find the answer?

(a)   The boy mentions "un cadeau" – a *present*. It's for "pour la Fête des Mères" – hopefully you will recognise "mères" – *mothers. It's for* **Mother's Day**. Towards the end of the conversation the woman says "je suis sûre que votre mère les appréciera".

(b)   The price is **huit** euros **soixante** – **€8.60**.

Fourth Conversation

> 4   **(a)**   What did Isabelle do at the weekend?
>
>   **(b)**   What is she going to buy tomorrow (**one item**)?

How do you find the answer?

(a)   Isabelle tells her friend "J'ai **décoré ma chambre**" – "décoré" sounds quite like its English equivalent, "*decorated*" and you will recognise "*chambre*" – *bedroom*. She says "je l'ai **peinte** en **vert**" – *she painted it green* and "j'ai aussi **changé** les **rideaux**" – *I changed the curtains*. Any of these answers is correct.

> **To do!**
>
> *REVISE WISE / POINTS TO NOTE*
>
> You can find these items and other items of furniture in the **Vocabulary Revision Lists**, page 154.

(b)   "quelques nouveaux **meubles**" – *furniture*. Since it's a bedroom she mentions "un **lit**" – *a bed*, "une **chaise**" – *a chair* and "une **armoire**" – *a wardrobe*. Any **one** of these items.

Fifth Conversation

5   (a)   To which country is Jean-Luc's brother going?

      (b)   Why can't Virginie go to the party on Sunday evening?

How do you find the answer?

(a) Jean-Luc says that his brother "part en échange **en Ecosse**" – he's going to *Scotland*.

(b) Virgine says she won't be able to go to the party because "nous allons passer dimanche **chez mes grands-parents**" – *spending Sunday at her grandparents*, "et nous serons **de retour très tard le soir**" – *we'll be back too/very late in the evening*.

To do!

Revise the names of countries, page 157.

REVISE WISE
POINTS TO NOTE

Section D

- **Section D** usually consists of a conversation between two young people, one male, one female. In 2009 this is the case – Claire is talking to Martin.
- This section is always set out in **segments**, and 2009 followed this pattern. The recording is played three times
- There are **two or three questions** to each segment
- The first time, the conversation is played right through, the second time in **four segments with pauses** after each segment and finally right through again.
- Don't try to write your answer during the first playing. Just make notes. Wait until the pauses during the second playing to write your answer.

Claire is talking to Martin. You will hear their conversation **three times**, first in full, then in **four segments** with pauses after each segment and finally right through again. Answer the questions below.

First Segment

1. (a) Where does Claire say she is going?
   (b) Why is Martin unable to go with her?

How do you find the answer?

(a) Claire says "je vais à la boulangerie" – *I'm going to the bakers/bakery*.

(b) Martin says "je suis **pressé**" – *I'm in a hurry*; "**Le vétérinaire** avec mon nouveau chien" – "Le vétérinaire" sounds quite like the English word "*vet*" and the word "chien" (*a dog*) is easy. The answer is "*He is going to the vet with his new dog*".

To do!

Revise the names for the various shops from the Vocabulary Revision Lists, pages 152/153.

REVISE WISE — POINTS TO NOTE

Second Segment

2. (a) According to Martin, who chose the dog's unusual name, *Banane*?
   (b) Give the following details about the dog:
      (i) His colour   (ii) His age

How do you find the answer?

(a) Martin remarks that the dog's name is "bizarre" – strange or funny and says "C'est **ma petite soeur** qui a choisi le nom" – *his little sister chose the name*.

(b) (i) Claire says "il est tout **noir**" – all *black*.
    (ii) Be careful here ! The dog "a seulement **neuf mois**" – *nine months* – Claire remarks that he is "petit" – *small*.

Third Segment

3. (a) What part of the dog's body is injured?
    (b) What was the dog doing when the injury happened?
    (c) When does Claire say she will telephone Martin?

How do you find the answer?

(a) Martin says "il s'est coupé l'oreille gauche" – *his left* ear. A little further on Claire says "cette blessure à l'oreille semble assez sérieuse" – so you will hear *ear* mentioned again.

> **To do!**
>
> Revise the words for parts of the body in the **Vocabulary Revision Lists**, page 148.
>
> *REVISE WISE — POINTS TO NOTE*

(b) "Quand il **jouait dans le jardin**" – *when* **he was playing** *in the garden*.

(c) Claire says "je te téléphonerai **ce soir**" – ***this evening/tonight***.

Fourth Segment

4. (a) Why did Martin's parents give him a new mobile phone?
    (b) Write in the rest of Martin's mobile phone number.

How do you find the answer?

(a) Martin says "grâce aux **bonnes notes** que j'ai reçues dans mon **bulletin scolaire**" – *thanks to* **the good marks** *I got in my* **school report**.

(b) Martin gives Claire his number and then Claire repeats it. As you will hear this segment three times, you will, in fact, hear the numbers six times! He says 06.58. dix-sept – 17; trente-neuf – 39 – quarante et un – 41. The number is **06.58.17.39.41**.

Section E

- The fifth section, **Section E**, consists of **news items**.
- There are usually five. The final item is usually a **weather forecast**.
- Each news item is **separate** and usually consists of **two questions**.
- You will hear each item **twice**.

> **To do!**
>
> *REVISE WISE — POINTS TO NOTE*
>
> Prepare for this final question by revising words and phrases for weather from the **Vocabulary Revision Lists**, page 158.

First Item

1. (a) How long will the international maritime festival in Calais last?
   (b) At what time will the opening ceremony begin?

How do you find the answer?

(a) The news item says "durant **une semaine**" – *for* **a** *week*.

(b) You are listening for a time – you will hear "la cérémonie d'ouverture commence à **20 heures**" – You may answer *20 hours/8 o'clock/ 8 p.m./20.00*.

Second Item

2. (a) Which sport is mentioned in this item?
   (b) Which country defeated France last Wednesday?

How do you find the answer?

(a) This was very straight-forward. The news reader says "Championnat de basket" – *basketball*.

(b) The team which defeated France is mentioned twice – "**Pays Bas**" – the *Netherlands* or *Holland*.

> **To do!**
>
> *REVISE WISE — POINTS TO NOTE*
>
> Revise the name of countries from the **Vocabulary Revision Lists**, page 157.

Third Item

3. **(a)** Name **two** types of vehicle involved in the accident

   (i)   (ii)

How do you find the answer?

(a) (i)   The newsreader says it was "un accident de la route" – *a road accident*, this may help you.

(ii)   The vehicles involved were "**une camionnette**" – *a van* and "**une moto**", *a motorbike*. Remember "moto" is not a car!

To do!

Revise the names of vehicles in the **Vocabulary Revision Lists**, page 159, les Transports.

Fourth Item

4. **(a)** How many students marched in the streets of Lyon?

   (b) What were they protesting about?

How do you find the answer?

(a)   The newsreader says there were "**trois cent**" – *300* "**cinquante**" – *50*, so *350*.

(b)   "ils protestent" – is very like the English, "la mauvaise **qualité** de la **nourriture** servie **à la cantine** de leur école" – *the (bad) quality of the food in the school canteen.*

Fifth Item

To do!

If you haven't already done so, you should thoroughly revise all the words associated with the weather, as there is nearly always a question involving a weather forecast, see the Vocabulary Revision Lists, page 158.

REVISE WISE *POINTS TO NOTE*

5   From the list of words given below, select **one** word which best describes the weather in **each** of the areas mentioned.

Cloudy – Warm – Rainy – Foggy – Windy – Cold

(i)   Northern France   _____

(ii)   Western France   _____

How do you find the answer?

(i)   "Dans l'**Ouest** de la France" is the West of France. The newsreader says it will be "très mauvais, il **pleuvra** toute la journée" – *rainy*.

(ii)   "Dans **le Sud** de la France" is the South of France. "Il fera **froid**" – *cold*. Also it says the temperature will be "autour de 5 degrés" – which is 5 degrees.

Section II: Reading Comprehension

Question 1

(a) You want to return a book to the library during your stay in France. Which of the following signs would you look for?

(*a*) Maison de la Presse   (*b*) Papeterie   (*c*) Bibliothèque
(*d*) Marchand de journaux

How do you find the answer?

If you are not immediately sure of the answer, look at the **four** options carefully.
(*a*) contains the word Presse, so it probably relates to *newspapers*.
(*b*) Papeterie is like the English word *paper*. It is a shop that sells stationery and paper products.
(*d*) Marchand de Journaux contains the word "journaux" (plural of the word "journal") meaning *newspapers*. Marchand is a *merchant* or *seller*, so this is a *newsagent*.
This leaves you with (c) Bibliothèque – a *library*. Remember the Bible is a book !
Answer: **(c)**

To do!

Revise names for shops and buildings in your **Vocabulary Revision Lists** on pages 152/153.

REVISE WISE
POINTS TO NOTE

(b) You are in a French railway station and you want to buy a train ticket. Which of these would you look for?

(*a*) Consigne   (*b*) Guichet   (*c*) Accès aux quais   (*d*) Buffet

How do you find the answer?

If you are not immediately sure of the answer, look at the **four** options carefully
The vocabulary needed here relates to the railway station.
(*a*) Consigne means *lockers*
(*c*) Accès aux quais – means *the way (accès) to the platforms (quais)*
(*d*) Buffet like the English word "*buffet*", means *food counter*
This leaves you with (b) Guichet – *ticket office or counter*
Answer: **(b)**

To do!

You can revise this vocabulary in **Vocabulary Revision Lists**, on page 151.

REVISE WISE
POINTS TO NOTE

Question 2

The second question is a recipe for veal (calf meat). A recipe often comes up on the paper.

(a) *Flour, sugar, egg, lemon.* Which one of these four is **not** listed in the ingredients?

(b) What direction is given in **point 3** of the cooking ingredients?

(c) How should this dish be served?

How do you find the answer?

(a) You have to find the ingredient which is **not** mentioned. Look at the list of ingredients and see which ones you can find.
- *Flour* is farine. This **is** on the list
- *Egg* is oeuf, and jaune is *yellow.* You can work out that this is *egg yolk.* This **is** on the list
- *Lemon* is citron – lemon is a citrus fruit. This **is** on the list.

The word *sugar* is not on the list (since it a savoury recipe, this would be unlikely!), so this is the answer.

(b) You are asked what direction is given in **point 3** of the instructions. The answer is "**ajouter**" – *add* **deux ou trois verres** – *two or three glasses* – d'eau – *water*. Be careful with your answer, as 1 point is deducted if you leave out the amount of water (*two or three glasses*)

(c) You are asked how the dish should be served. In **Point 9** you will see "**servir**" (*serve*) au **riz** – with *rice*.

Question 3

- Read **the heading** above the passage as this helps you to understand what it is about. This tells you the passage contains advice for young people regarding part-time jobs.
- "**Ados**" is short for adolescents
- The picture shows a young girl holding a pizza in a pizza restaurant.

(a) Write down **one** reason why you may want to earn money. (**Part 1**)

(b) State **one** thing that you will discover by working during the holidays. (**Part 1**)

(c) Name **one** way you can find a summer job. (**Part 2**)

How do you find the answer?

(a) Look carefully at the first paragraph. The answers to the first 2 questions are found there. "Parce que.." means *because*, so what follows is the answer. It says "tu rêves de **partir en vacances**" – *go on holidays* and "**acheter une console de jeux**" – *to buy a games console*.

(a) The word "découvrir" means *to discover*, so what follows is the answer "**le sens de la responsabilité**" *a sense of responsibility* and "**la nécessité**" – *the need* – "**de respecter les horaires**" – *to be keep to a timetable/need to be on time*.

(a) There are 3 possible answers. Look for the verb "trouver", which means "*to find*".
  - The words "Agence pour l'emploi", means "*employment agency*";
  - "s'informant à **la Mairie**" – *asking at the Town Hall*;
  - "en discutant avec **les amis**" – *talking to friends / through friends*.
  Any one of these three possibilities will give you the marks.

Question 4

● This is a typical question as you have a selection of **seven** short extracts with 4 questions.

The following extracts are taken from a recommended reading list for French teenagers. Each consists of a short summary of a book. Read the extracts and answer the questions.

> Write the **name of the book** which tells the story of someone who
> **(a)** is very close to his / her grandfather
> **(b)** loves working with horses
> **(c)** has received a Valentine's Day card
> **(d)** has a friend who is moving to the seaside

How do you find the answer?

Firstly, jot down the key words you need for each question
(a) *grandfather* = grand-père
(b) *horses* = cheval/chevaux
(c) *Valentine's Day card* = carte de Saint Valentin
(d) *to move house* = déménager; *seaside* = au bord de la mer

Now try to find these key words in the summaries
(a) **grandpère** – In "**C'est tout de suite le soir**" you will see the keyword "grand-père" and the verb "adorer", so we know that Myrtho loves her grandfather. This is the answer to **(a)**.
(b) **chevaux** – In "**La route du nord**" there is a picture of a girl on a horse. However, do not make your decision based on this. Check the text as well. In the second line you can read "**travailler** avec **les chevaux**" – *work with horses*. This is the answer to **(b)**
(c) **carte de Saint Valentin** – in the first summary "**Susie la chipie**" you can read in the second line "magnifique **carte de 'Saint Valentin'**". This is the answer for **(c)**
(d) **déménager** and **au bord de la mer** – in the summary "**Adieu, mes douze ans**", you will find in the last two lines "**déménager** et s'installer dans un petit village **au bord de la mer**". This is the answer for **(d)**

Question 5

- Again always read the line above the passage directly beside the question number as this helps you to understand what the passage is about. In this question 4 young people say how they feel about secondary school.
- There are 4 parts and each comment follows the name of the student so it is very straightforward as you know exactly where to find each answer.

> **(a)** **Oscar** says that you learn things about life at school. What example does he give?
>
> **(b)** How does **Manon** suggest reorganising the timetable?
>
> **(c)** According to **Thomas**, what subject does he find relaxing?
>
> **(d)** How does **Sandra** describe the walls in her school?

How do you find the answer?

(a) In part 1 Oscar says that at school "on apprend – *(one learns)* sur la vie, **les dangers du tabac, par exemple**". The word "dangers" is the same as English and "tabac" is very like the English word "*tobacco*". The answer is *the risks/dangers of smoking/tobacco*.

(b) In part 2, Manon mentions the words "emploi du temps au collège" – *school timetable*. Her suggestion is in the last sentence – "et pourqoui pas **commencer les cours à 10 h** tous les matins ?" "*Pourquoi pas*", tells us she is saying "*why not …*"?; "commencer" is like the English word "*commence/start*" ; "les cours" – *classes*; 10h – the h tells us that this is a time. She suggests *that classes should start at 10 every morning*.

(c) This is a little more difficult if you do not know the French word for "*relaxing*", but it is not impossible to find the answer. Thomas mentions several school subjects, but they are "utiles" – *useful* (the English words "utility" or "to utilise" might help you). You are left with "Avec le dessin, … on se détend, ….. and "on a besoin de faire du sport". "Avoir besoin de" means *to need*, so the answer is not sport. This leaves you with "dessin" – a bit like the English word *design*, and it means drawing or art. The answer is *drawing/art class*.

(d) In part 4, you have to find out **one point** that Sandra says about the walls in her school. There are in fact four possible answers. The key word is "**mur**" – wall. She describes "des **murs bruns** avec de **l'encre** et des **graffitis**. Ils sont **si sales**."
- "Brun" is *brown*;
- "encre" is "*ink*" and
- "graffitis" is the same as the English word.
- They are "si sales" – *so dirty*. As you only need to give one point, you do not need to be able to translate all the possibilities. Any one of the following is the correct answer
  - *the walls are brown*;
  - *covered in ink/there's ink on them*;
  - *there's graffiti on them*;
  - *they are dirty*.

Question 6

- This question has no information beside the question to help you understand what it is about. Read the French title carefully *Un taureau dans la maison.*

- *La Maison* means the house and this word should cause no difficulties! The picture of a bull will help you to understand the article. There are 2 parts and each part requires 2 answers. Always be careful to read the questions carefully and only write the answer from the part as indicated.

(a) What was Joëlle doing when she heard the noise in the kitchen? (**Part 1**)

(b) Why had Joëlle's husband gone out? (**Part 1**)

(c) The bull damaged some items in the house. Name **two** of them. (**Part 2**)

How do you find the answer?

(a) In part 1 in the second line you can find the word "prend **une douche**" – *taking a shower.* In the fourth line it also says "elle sort de la salle de bains" – *she was coming out of the bathroom.* The answer is: **having a shower** (in the bathroom)

(b) This answer is also in part 1. "Mari" is the word for *husband.* You can see that he "parti quelques minutes plus tôt **faire des courses**" – *to do the shopping.* The answer is: ***to do the shopping/messages/buy food***

(c) The answer is in Part 3. There are three items mentioned and you are asked to name **two** of them. "le réfrigérateur" is easy enough. The other two are "l'aspirateur" – ***the hoover/vacuum cleaner*** and "le lave-vaisselle" – ***the dish-washer*** (laver = *to wash*, vaisselle = *the dishes*)

Question 7

- This question has 3 sections with **5 questions**. Each question tells you where the answer is to be found.
- The information is given beside the question number, telling you that this is taken from a tourist website about Monaco. There is a picture also and a title **Principauté de Monaco**.

> **(a)** Where exactly, according to the text, is the Principality of Monaco situated? (**Part 1**)
>
> **(b)** For how long has the history of Monaco been associated with the Grimaldi family? (**Part 1**)
>
> **(c)** Apart from French and Monegù, name **one** language which is spoken in Monaco. (**Part 2**)
>
> **(d)** Name the **two** groups of people who receive gifts on the national holiday. (**Part 3**)
>
> **(e)** What takes place on the evening of 19th November each year? (**Part 3**)

How do you find the answer?

(a) You are told the answer is in **part 1**. There are two elements to the answer and to gain maximum points you must write the two elements. "Situé" means *situated*, so this is where you find your answers

- "**aux pieds** des **Alpes** du Sud et **bordant la Méditerranée**". "pied" is the French word for "*foot*", and you must use this phrase. ("in the Alps" in not correct and will earn you no marks) So be careful to give the full phrase;
- "*bordant*" looks like the word "*border*", so the second element is *bordering/beside the Mediterranean*.

The full answer is: ***at the foot of the (southern) Alps, beside the Mediterranean***.

(b) This answer is also in **part 1**. You will probably recognise "histoire" as history. You are now looking for a time or number of years. "Sept cent ans" – *700 years*.

(c) You will see at the start of part 2 that the official language is French. And then two other languages are mentioned "l'italien" – *Italian* and "l'anglais" – *English*. The answer is either ***Italian or English***.

(d) The answers to the next question are to be found in part 3. "cadeaux" is the French for *present/gift*. You can read "la distribution de cadeaux **aux pauvres** – *the poor* ... et **aux malades** – *the sick*".

(e) The final sentence begins with "le soir" – *in the evening*, so this is your answer. "il y a **un grand feu d'artifice**". You need to know this word to give the correct answer – ***a big fireworks display***.

Question 8

- A full page with an article and 6 questions.
- No information is given beside the question number; only the instructions.
- The title is a woman's name and there is a picture of a young woman.

(a) What job was Sheryfa training for before she began her musical career? (**Part 1**)

(b) When was her new album *"Vénus"* released? (**Part 1**)

(c) According to Sheryfa, what are her songs about? (**one point**) (**Part 2**)

(d) What does Sheryfa say she always does? (**Part 3**)

(e) Why did Sheryfa and her first boyfriend split up? (**Part 4**)

(f) Where precisely does Sheryfa want to spend her holidays with her son? (**Part 5**)

How do you find the answer?

(a) The word "avant" means "*before*", so you know you will find the answer here. You can read that Sheryfa "suivait une formation d'apprentie **coiffeuse**". This means *hairdresser*.

(b) You must give an exact answer here to gain maximum marks. "Son nouvel album *"Vénus"* est sorti **à la fin de l'année dernière**" – at *the end of last year* (if you write "last year", you only get 1 mark)

(c) The answer is in **part 2**. She speaks of "mes **joies** et mes **difficultés**". Both words are like their English meanings – her *joys* and her *difficulties*. You just need to mention one.

(d) You are looking for something she always does – faire = *to do* and toujours = *always*. She says "je fais toujours **ce que je veux quand je veux**". "je veux" means "*I want*", so the answer is *she does what she wants when she wants*. You must give the full answer here.

(e) In **part 4** she describes her first relationship. But "nous nous sommes séparés – *they separated*… quand il est parti **faire des études à l'université**" – *when he went away to study at university*. You get no marks for saying he went away.

(f) You need to find a place or location where she wants to spend her holidays (vacances). In the second line of **part 5** she says "j'ai envie de partir en vacances **à la plage** avec lui". *To the beach* is the answer.

127

Question 9

- The **final question** is similar to previous years. The interview takes up a **full page**. This is an interview with a famous French rally driver. There are 6 questions with some questions requiring 2 answers so in fact there are **8 answers needed.**
- There is a small photo of the rally driver. The interview is divided into **6 parts.**

(a) Why is Sébastien considered to be one of the greatest French sportsmen? (**Part 1**)

(b) Why did Sébastien and his wife decide to live in Mont-sur-Rolle? (**Part 2**)

(c) Name **one** benefit of living in Switzerland which Sébastien mentions. (**Part 3**)

(d) Write down **two** comments which Sébastien makes about fatherhood. (**Part 4**)

(e) Why does Sébastien say that he is lucky? (**Part 5**)

(f) What does Sébastien say about his everyday driving habits? (**Two details**) (**Part 6**)

How do you find the answer?

(a) You know the answer is in part 1. A sportsperson is "un sportif", so if you can find this you will find the answer nearby.

- Firstly the text says he is "**le pilote le plus titré de l'histoire**" – pilote in this case means a *driver* – le plus titré, *the most titled in history*.
- The text also says "Sébastien **a remporté le championnat du monde des rallyes cinq fois** entre 2004 et 2008". "Remporter" is the verb *"to win/carry off"*. *He has won the world rallying championship* – how many times? "**cinq fois**" – *five times between 2004 and 2008*.

(b) Look for the verb "choisir" – *to choose/to pick*. In the second line you will see "nous avons choisi cet endroit **parce que nous avons toujours voulu habiter au bord d'un lac**" – **they always wanted to live beside a lake.**

(c) You are looking for **one** benefit of living in Switzerland. There are two mentioned.

- "**La tranquillité** de la campagne" is the first answer – *the calm of the countryside*.
- "La **proximité** (nearness) de la **grande ville** de Genève" – *being near the large town of Geneva*. Either of these will give you full marks.

(d) You will find your answer in **Part** 4. There are four comments in the paragraph.

- Firstly he says "elle n'a pas changé grand-chose à ce que je suis" – *it hasn't changed him*.
- "J'ai toujours envie de voir ma fille, Valentine" – "envie" is *want*, so he says *he always wants to see his daughter*.
- "A cinq heures, je me lève pour lui donner à boire" – he says *he gets up at 5 o'clock to give her something to drink/to feed her*
- And finally, you can find "je sors beaucoup moins avec mes copains qu'avant" – *he goes out much less with his friends*

(e) The French word for *luck* is "chance". In the first line of part 5, you will see "j'ai de la chance de pouvoir faire un métier que j'adore" – I'm lucky to be able to do a job (métier) which I love – *he has a job he loves*.

(f) You are looking for two details about his everyday driving habits. In the text he says three things.

- "Je respecte les limitations de vitesse" – you may recognize the word "vite" – *fast* in vitesse. So what does he respect? – *the limits of fastness* – *he respects the speed limits*
- Secondly he says "je mets *(put on)* toujours ma ceinture de sécurité" – something to do with security – his safety belt – *he always wears his seat belt*.
- The third thing is a little harder. You need to know the words "décontracté" – *relaxed*, and "au volant" – *at the wheel*. *He is relaxed at the wheel/when driving*

Section III: Written Expression

Answer both (a) and (b)   (80 marks)

(a) You are on a school tour to Paris with your class. Write a postcard to your French penpal Camille. In your card tell her
- where you are and who you are with
- that you went to a museum yesterday
- that you will visit Fontainebleau on Tuesday

Remember...
- Use the correct **format**, although you are not rewarded marks
- You must attempt all **three tasks** (see pages 86–89 for expressions)
- A good **knowledge of tenses** is important (see pages 91–106)

Sample postcard

Opening salutation – correct spelling is required

> Paris le deux avril
>
> Salut Camille
>
> Un grand bonjour de Paris. Je suis arrivée ici hier avec ma classe. Je m'amuse bien.
>
> Je suis allée au musée hier. C'était intéressant.
>
> Je visiterai le château à Fontainebleau mardi. Nous voyagerons en autocar.
>
> Dis « bonjour » à tout le monde de ma part.
>
> À bientôt
>
> **Kate.**

1st Task: Past Tense

2nd Task: Past Tense

3rd Task: Future Tense

Closing salutation – correct spelling is required

(b) You have just gone back to school after the Christmas holidays. Your French penpal Philippe has sent you a Christmas present. Write a letter in French to Philippe. In your letter
– thank him for his letter and the present
– tell him what you did during the Christmas holidays
– give him some news about your best friend
– tell him about your plans for your birthday
– ask him to come and visit you next summer

Opening salutation – correct spelling is required

Date: No capital letter for the month

Galway, le 12 janvier

Cher Philippe,

Merci mille fois pour ta lettre et pour le CD. Quelle surprise ! Le CD est super. Je l'écoute tous les jours.

1st Task: Present Tense

2nd Task: Past Tense

Pendant les vacances, j'ai fait la grasse matinée presque chaque jour. C'était formidable ! J'ai rencontré mes amis et nous avons regardé des DVDs dans le salon. Bien sûr, je suis allée aux magasins. Les soldes étaient très super. J'ai acheté des vêtements.

3rd Task: Past Tense

L'anniversaire de ma meilleure amie Patricia était samedi dernier. C'était chouette. La fête a commencé à neuf heures et a fini à minuit. Tout le monde a bavardé et a dansé. Mon père est venu me chercher.

Je voudrais un nouveau portable ou ipod pour mon anniversaire. Donc, je ne veux pas avoir de boum. Je prendrai un repas au restaurant avec ma famille. Ça sera ennuyeux mais j'ai besoin d'un portable !

4th Task: Future Tense

5th Task: Present Tense

Est-ce que tu veux venir en Irlande l'été prochain ? Il y a beaucoup à faire ici. Nous pouvons faire de la natation à la piscine, faire du vélo et bien sûr tu peux rencontrer mes copains.

Écris-moi vite pour me donner de tes nouvelles.

Amitiés

Closing salutation – correct spelling is required

Evelyn

Remember...

REVISE WISE POINTS TO NOTE

- **Format** for the **month**; use "**cher**" for the opening salutation (**chère** if you are writing to a girl); use **Amitiés/Amicalement** for the closing salutation
- Attempt the **five tasks** asked. **Expand** a point where possible
- Knowledge of **tenses** is important (see pages 91–105)

Answers – Were You Right?

Listening Comprehension Section

Track 1   (b)   Cancelling a booking

Track 2   (c)   Suggesting an outing

Track 3   (c)   Saying they are not well

Track 4   (b)   Looking for a lost item

Track 5   (a)   Post office

Track 6   (c)   Tourist office

Track 7   (c)   Railway station

Track 8   (b)   Petrol station

Track 9

	Name	Jérôme Lejeune
1	His age	16 years old
2	Where he lives (**one** point)	A detached house/beside the sea/in Finistère
3	Number of sisters	Three
4	**Two** of his hobbies	Sailing/Swimming/Water-skiing
5	Where he goes on holidays	His grandparents' farm in Normandy
6	What he does while he is there (**one** point)	He helps his granddad with the animals or he goes horse-riding
7	His future career	Vet

132

🎧 **Track** 10

Name		Florentine Rocher
1	Her birthday	10 May
2	Country where she was born	Belgium
3	Colour of eyes	Blue
4	Colour of hair	Red
5	Musical instrument played by her	Violin
6	**Two** subjects she likes at school	Geography/Art/Music
7	**One** animal she dislikes	Her friend's parrot/Her brother's white mice

🎧 **Track** 11

1 I live at 13 rue de la gare.
2 This book costs €10.50.
3 My telephone number is 01.66.42.31.55.
4 I will take 2 kilos.
5 Read conversation on page 75.
6 The bus goes at 14.20 (or 2.20 pm).
7 My classes start at 8.10.
8 Do you have these shoes in red, size 37?
9 My address is apartment number 12, Résidence Marine.
10 A ticket for Nantes costs €5.

🎧 **Track** 12

The vowel sounds in French are:
a – e – i – o – u and y

🎧 **Track** 13

The consonants are:
b – c – d – f – g – h – j – k – l – m – n – p – q –r – s – t – v – w – x and z

🎧 **Track** 14

1	LAUNAY		4	LORIENT
2	BELLANGER		5	BEAULIEU
3	PIDOU		6	GUIGNEN

Track 15

Conversation 1

Where:	The swimming-pool
Directions:	Straight ahead, 2nd left. The pool is on the left, beside the cinema Rex.

Conversation 2

Where:	The bus station
Directions:	Turn right at the roundabout. Continue for 200 metres and it is facing you at the end of the street.

Conversation 3

Where:	The tourist office
Directions:	Cross the bridge, continue along by the park and the tourist office is on the corner of the square.

Track 16

Conversation 1

What is lost:	New runners/Sports shoes
Description:	Black and white

Conversation 2

What is lost:	A watch
Description:	Gold, black leather strap. A birthday present

Conversation 3

What is lost:	Keys
Description:	Two large keys and a car key

Conversation 4

What is lost:	Copy with English homework
Description:	Red, with name and class on the cover

Conversation 5

What is lost:	An umbrella
Description:	Large, red, blue and black

Track 17

Conversation 1

(a)	Type of accommodation:	One room
(b)	What facilities:	Shower and sea view
(c)	When:	Next weekend, 3 to 5 November (two nights)

Conversation 2

(a) How many rooms: Two rooms

(b) How many people: Four people

(c) What dates: Saturday 6 June until 13 June

Conversation 3

(a) Type of site: Site for a caravan

(b) How many people: Two adults, two children (four people)

(c) When: This evening

Track 18

Conversation 1

(a) How many people: Two people

(b) When: Next Thursday, 4 March

(c) What occasion: Granny's (80th) birthday

Conversation 2

(a) When: Saturday, 5 August

(b) How many people: Ten people

(c) What occasion: 25th wedding anniversary

Track 19

Conversation 1

	Woman	Man
Starter	Soup of the day	Tomato salad
Main course	Salmon	Lamb
Dessert	Lemon sorbet	Chocolate mousse
Drink	Bottle of white wine and a jug of water	

Conversation 2

	Woman	Man
Starter	Melon	Vegetable soup
Main course	Veal	Chicken
Dessert	Pear tart	Ice cream (vanilla/strawberry)
Drink	Bottle of house red wine and a jug of water	

135

Track 20

Conversation 1
Geography test – everything about Germany, climate, industries, rivers and mountains

Conversation 2
English homework – the exercises on page 63 – four in all

Conversation 3
Maths class – hates Maths, find them very difficult and teacher is very strict. Friend says he will help, and in return get help with his Spanish

Track 21

Conversation 1
Complaint:	Pain in stomach, vomiting all night
How long:	Two days
Advice given:	Drink lots, don't eat. If not better after 24 hours, ring for a prescription

Conversation 2
Complaint:	Stayed in sun for too long, now feels unwell
Symptoms:	Back completely red
Advice given:	Prescription for cream, drink a lot of water and stay out of the sun for two days

Conversation 3
Complaint:	Toothache, can't eat
How long:	Three days
Appointment for:	Come and see the dentist at midday

Track 22

First segment
Question 1	Arnaud has been in Montréal in Canada.
Question 2	He was helping his uncle in his supermarket.
Question 3	Two days ago (last Sunday)

Second segment
Question 4	Mélanie has been working in a crèche/nursery.
Question 5	She thinks she would like to be a primary school teacher and she wanted to see if she liked working with children.
Question 6	She has to go, her lunch-break is over/She has to go to work.

Third segment

Question 7	He suggests they meet for a coffee or a pizza and he will tell her about his experiences in Canada.
Question 8	She goes to aerobics classes on Wednesdays.
Question 9	Arnaud suggests they meet on Friday night (at 7.30).

Fourth segment

Question 10	He has an interview with the manager of the supermarket.
Question 11	He's looking for a part-time job/He needs money/He liked working in the supermarket in Canada.

Track 23

News item 1

What vehicles:	A lorry and a bicycle
Cause of accident:	Icy road
What happened to the young boy:	Boy taken to hospital

News item 2

How many vehicles:	Two cars
How the injured were brought to the hospital:	By helicopter
Cause of accident:	Fog

News item 3

What vehicles:	A bus and a van
Who helped at the scene:	A doctor
For how long was the road blocked:	An hour

Track 24

Robbery 1

When:	Sunday night
What was stolen:	€10,000
Getaway:	Old red lorry

Robbery 2

When:	About 8 pm yesterday evening
What was stolen:	Contents of cash register, about €8,500
Getaway:	Grey Peugeot car

Robbery 3

When:	Monday evening
What was stolen:	Mobile phone, CD player and about €25
Getaway:	Motorbike

Track 25

News Item 1
What happened:	Heavy rain/Floods
When:	Tuesday and Wednesday
Outcome:	Houses were flooded and residents of houses along the river were evacuated

News Item 2
What crops are threatened:	Apples and pears
How strong was the wind:	120 km/h
Cost of damage:	Farmers may lose €1 million

News Item 3
In what month:	July
Where is there a risk of fire:	Forest
What is forbidden:	Using fireworks
	Lighting fires in gardens and picnic areas

Track 26

Sports report 1
What sport is mentioned:	Rugby
Who won:	Scotland
Score:	Scotland: 30 – Italy: 15

Sports report 2
What sport is mentioned:	Football
Who won:	Morocco
Score:	Senegal: 2 – Morocco: 3

Sports report 3
What sport is mentioned:	Basketball
Who won:	Greece
Score:	Greece: 84 – Germany: 79

Track 27

Weather forecast 1
Type of weather expected:	Warm
Temperature(s):	23–30 degrees
Outlook:	Fine weather will continue

Weather forecast 2
Type of weather expected:	Northern France: Rain
	Mountain region: Snow
Outlook for tomorrow:	Cold weather will continue, low temperatures

Weather forecast 3

Type of weather expected: Strong winds
Temperature(s):   10 degrees

Reading Comprehension Section

Question 1 – Exercise 1

(a) (a) Salle de jeux
(b) (c) www.météo.fr

Question 1 – Exercise 2

(a) (c) Gendarmerie
(b) (d) Crêperie

Question 2 – Exercise 1

(a) For all ages
(b) Every day
(c) Every weekend (or by booking during the week)

Question 2 – Exercise 2

(a) July and August
(b) Saturday

Question 3 – Exercise 1

(c) Flour

Question 3 – Exercise 2

(a) (c) Windmills
(b) Other activities are swimming, bowls, children's games and
       table tennis.
(c) Families

Question 3 – Exercise 3

(a) Lemon
(b) 35 minutes
(c) Let them cool down/Put them in the fridge for two hours.

Question 4 – Exercise 1

(a) Antibes
(b) Nice Ville
(c) St. Laurent du Var
(d) Villefranche

Question 4 – Exercise 2

(a) La Chassagnette
(b) Les Saladelles
(c) La Farandole
(d) La Comédie

Question 4 – Exercise 3

1   21h30
2   20h55
3   20h45
4   21h00

Question 5 – Exercise 1

(a) Yesterday
(b) 16
(c) Public meetings

Question 6 – Exercise 1

(a) Tuesday morning
(b) Behind Mon. Rocher's house
(c) Emptied the pool/the vet gave the cow an injection/they raised the cow using a harness and tractor
(d) Because of her weight
(e) The cow had a calf

Question 7 – Exercise 1

(a) Nine mothers
(b) Four months
(c) The 81st patient to be admitted to hospital
(d) A neighbour

Question 8 – Exercise 1

(a) Third 100th birthday
(b) Her sister
(c) To house old people in the area
(d) Being re-united with all the family
(e) The family **and** all the people who took part in this great day.

Question 9 – Exercise 1

(a) Had to learn new language/adapt to new culture.
(b) They wanted to travel and help other people.
(c) At least 15 hours.
(d) Dressed in orange robes/walk barefoot/don't work/they meditate.
(e) They join their hands at face level.
(f) Pupils have to help find food for families.
(g) He helps his father in the fields/he cuts rice/he gathers dry wood for the stove/he catches crabs and frogs.
(h) He follows his favourite rugby club.

Question 9 – Exercise 2

(a) It is a big family.
(b) 1 Giving money is easier but it is a responsibility.
    2 To give without thinking is as serious as not giving at all.
(c) She hates to share the bill. She wants to pay.
(d) She likes when they have to pay to see her movies.
(e) She sold tee shirts and outfits she made herself, and she babysat.
(f) They never took any pocket money from their mother; they earned it themselves.
(g) Acting in some interesting films
(h) People who criticise artists who work for money

Grammar Section

Exercise 1

	passer *to spend*	jouer *to play*	rester *to stay*	arriver *to arrive*
je	pass**e**	jou**e**	rest**e**	arriv**e**
tu	pass**es**	jou**es**	rest**es**	arriv**es**
il/elle/on	pass**e**	jou**e**	rest**e**	arriv**e**
nous	pass**ons**	jou**ons**	rest**ons**	arriv**ons**
vous	pass**ez**	jou**ez**	rest**ez**	arriv**ez**
ils/elles	pass**ent**	jou**ent**	rest**ent**	arriv**ent**

Exercise 11

1	Nous buvons beaucoup d'eau.
2	Nous faisons de la voile tous les jours.
3	Nous pouvons voir la plage de notre fenêtre.
4	Il fait soleil.
5	Je dois partir maintenant.

Exercise 12

1	J'attends ta lettre avec impatience.	*I am looking forward to receiving your letter.*
2	Nous t'attendons devant le supermarché.	*We are waiting for you in front of the supermarket.*
3	Les vacances finissent dans trois jours.	*The holidays are over in three days.*
4	Ma tante répond régulièrement à mes lettres.	*My aunt replies regularly to my letters.*
5	Je choisis le restaurant ce soir.	*I choose the restaurant this evening.*

Exercise 13

1 vas-(tu) ; 2 (je) suis ; 3 (toute la famille) va ; 4 (je) cherche ; 5 (je) range ;
6 (mon père) a ; 7 (elle) est; 8 (mon frère) a ; 9 (il) s'appelle

Exercise 14

1 (je) passe ; 2 (il) fait ; 3 (je) fais ; 4 (je) m'amuse ; 5 (je) visite ;
6 (je) rentre

Exercise 15

1 (j')ai passé ; 2 (il) a fait ; 3 (nous) sommes restés ; 4 (j')ai fait ;
5 (j')ai fait ; 6 (je) me suis [...] amusée

Exercise 16

	passer *to spend*	jouer *to play*	rester *to stay*	arriver *to arrive*
je	passerai	jouerai	resterai	arriverai
tu	passeras	joueras	resteras	arriveras
il/elle/on	passera	jouera	restera	arrivera
nous	passerons	jouerons	resterons	arriverons
vous	passerez	jouerez	resterez	arriverez
ils/elles	passeront	joueront	resteront	arriveront

Exercise 17

	louer *to hire/to rent*	retourner *to return*	visiter *to visit*	regarder *to look at*
je	louerai	retournerai	visiterai	regarderai
tu	loueras	retourneras	visiteras	regarderas
il/elle/on	louera	retournera	visitera	regardera
nous	louerons	retournerons	visiterons	regarderons
vous	louerez	retournerez	visiterez	regarderez
ils/elles	loueront	retourneront	visiteront	regarderont

Exercise 18

	finir *to finish*	partir *to leave*	sortir *to go out*	choisir *to choose*
je	finirai	partirai	sortirai	choisirai
tu	finiras	partiras	sortiras	choisiras
il/elle/on	finira	partira	sortira	choisira
nous	finirons	partirons	sortirons	choisirons
vous	finirez	partirez	sortirez	choisirez
ils/elles	finiront	partiront	sortiront	choisiront

Exercise 19

1. Nous resterons ici pendant deux semaines. *We will stay here for two weeks.*
2. Tu visiteras un château lundi prochain. *You will visit a castle next Monday.*
3. Ma famille et moi retournerons en Irlande la semaine prochaine. *My family and I will return to Ireland next week.*
4. Ma sœur finira ses devoirs demain. *My sister will finish her homework tomorrow.*
5. Je choisirai un restaurant pour le repas. *I will choose a restaurant for the meal.*

Exercise 20

1. Je serai de retour à huit heures. *I will be back at eight o'clock.*
2. Nous ferons une excursion demain. *We will go on an excursion tomorrow.*
3. Elle ira au marché samedi. *She will go to the market on Saturday.*
4. Ils auront des vacances en juillet. *They will have holidays in July.*
5. Je te verrai plus tard. *I will see you later.*
6. Nous pourrons faire du shopping ensemble. *We will be able to go shopping together.*
7. Est-ce que tu viendras nous voir bientôt ? *Will you come to see us soon?*
8. Pierre et Luc, vous devrez être au café à neuf heures. *Pierre and Luc, you will have to be at the café at nine o'clock.*

Exercise 21

1 Mon/Ton/Notre hôtel est au bord de la mer.	My//Your/Our hotel is beside the sea.
2 Mon/Ton/Notre camping est grand.	My/Your/Our campsite is big.
3 Je rencontre mes amis chaque jour.	I meet my friends every day.
4 Je reste dans un gîte avec ma famille pour deux semaines.	I am staying in a summer house with my family for two weeks.
5 Mon/Notre prof organise un voyage scolaire à Londres.	My/Our teacher is organising a school trip to London.
6 Comment se passent tes/vos vacances ?	How are your holidays going?
7 Mon père va bien.	My dad is well.
8 Mes amis s'amusent beaucoup ici.	My friends are having a lot of fun here.
9 Comment vont tes/vos parents?	How are your parents?
10 Mon/Notre vol est le deux juillet à trois heures.	My/Our flight is on the second of July at three o'clock.

 Exercise 22

	masculine	feminine	masculine plural	feminine plural
boring	ennuy**eux**	ennuy**euse**	ennuy**eux**	ennuy**euses**
old	vi**eux**/vi**eil**	vi**eille**	vi**eux**	vi**eilles**
nice	genti**l**	genti**lle**	genti**ls**	genti**lles**
small	peti**t**	peti**te**	peti**ts**	peti**tes**
serious	séri**eux**	séri**euse**	séri**eux**	séri**euses**
aggressive	agress**if**	agress**ive**	agress**ifs**	agress**ives**

 Exercise 23

1 La maison est bleue et noire.	The house is blue and black.
2 La fille est grande et jolie.	The girl is tall and pretty.
3 Les chaises sont petites et noires.	The chairs are small and black.
4 Marie est heureuse au lycée.	Marie is happy in school.
5 La semaine dernière, je suis allé(e) à Wexford.	Last week I went to Wexford.
6 Le mois dernier, il a visité l'Irlande.	Last month he visited Ireland.
7 Michelle est sportive et mignonne.	Michelle is sporty and cute.
8 « Je suis moyenne en maths et je suis forte en français », dit Claire.	'I am average at Maths and I am good at French', said Claire.
9 J'ai passé une longue journée au lycée.	I spent a long day in school.
10 Ma grand-mère est vieille.	My grandmother is old.

Les animaux (*Animals*)

l'agneau (m)	*lamb*
l'âne (m)	*donkey*
le boeuf	*ox*
le canard	*duck*
le caneton	*duckling*
le cerf	*deer*
le chat	*cat*
le chaton	*kitten*
le cheval	*horse*
la chèvre	*goat*
le chien	*dog*
le chiot	*puppy*
le cochon	*pig*
le cochon d'Inde	*guinea pig*
le cochonnet	*piglet*
le cygne	*swan*
le dauphin	*dolphin*
la dinde	*turkey*
l'éléphant (m)	*elephant*
la girafe	*giraffe*
la grenouille	*frog*
le kangourou	*kangaroo*
le lapin	*rabbit*
le lion	*lion*
le mouton	*sheep*
l'oie (f)	*goose*
l'oiseau (m)	*bird*
l'ours(e) (m/f)	*bear*
l'ourson (m)	*bear cub*
le perroquet	*parrot*
la perruche	*parakeet/budgie*
le poisson	*fish*
le poisson rouge	*gold-fish*
le poney	*pony*
la poule	*hen*
le poulet	*chicken*
le poussin	*chick*
le serpent	*snake*
le singe	*monkey*

la tortue	*tortoise*
la tortue de mer	*turtle*
la vache	*cow*

Le camping (*Campsite*)

l'accueil (m)	*reception desk/area*
l'aire de jeux (f)	*play area*
l'animateur/ l'animatrice (m/f)	*entertainer*
la caravane	*caravan*
l'emplacement (m)	*site*
la garderie	*nursery*
la laverie	*laundry*
le mobile home	*mobile/trailer*
le plat à emporter	*take-away food*
la salle de jeux	*games room*
la salle de séjour	*common room*
le tableau d'affichage	*notice board*
la tente	*tent*

Les chiffres (*Numbers*)

un	*one*
deux	*two*
trois	*three*
quatre	*four*
cinq	*five*
six	*six*
sept	*seven*
huit	*eight*
neuf	*nine*
dix	*ten*
onze	*eleven*
douze	*twelve*
treize	*thirteen*
quatorze	*fourteen*
quinze	*fifteen*
seize	*sixteen*
dix-sept	*seventeen*

dix-huit	*eighteen*
dix-neuf	*nineteen*
vingt	*twenty*
vingt-et-un	*twenty-one*
trente	*thirty*
quarante	*forty*
cinquante	*fifty*
soixante	*sixty*
soixante-dix	*seventy*
quatre-vingts	*eighty*
quatre-vingt-six	*eighty-six*
quatre-vingt-dix	*ninety*
cent	*hundred*
mille	*thousand*
un million	*a million*
un milliard	*a billion*
le/la premier/ière	*the first*
le/la deuxième	*the second*
le/la troisième	*the third*
le/la quatrième	*the fourth*
le quart	*quarter*
le tiers	*third*
la moitié	*half*
les trois-quarts	*three quarters*
le demi	*half*

'–aine' can be added to the end of any counting number, e.g.

une douz**aine**	*a dozen*
une vingt**aine**	*about twenty*
une cent**aine**	*about one hundred*

Le corps (Body)

les amygdales	*tonsils*
l'appendice (m)	*appendix*
la bouche	*mouth*
le bras	*arm*
la cheville	*ankle*
le cœur	*heart*
le cou	*neck*
le coude	*elbow*
les dents	*teeth*
le derrière	*bottom*
le doigt	*finger*
l'épaule (f)	*shoulder*
l'estomac (m)	*stomach*
le front	*forehead*

le genou	*knee*
la gorge	*throat*
la jambe	*leg*
la langue	*tongue*
les lèvres (f)	*lips*
la main	*hand*
le nez	*nose*
l'œil (m)	*eye*
l'ongle (m)	*nail*
l'oreille (f)	*ear*
l'orteil (m)	*toe*
le pied	*foot*
le poignet	*wrist*
la poitrine	*chest*
le pouce	*thumb*
le poumon	*lung*
la tête	*head*
le ventre	*stomach*
les yeux (m)	*eyes*

Les couleurs (Colours)

blanc/blanche	*white*
bleu(e)	*blue*
blond(e)	*blond/fair*
brun(e)	*brown*
clair(e)	*bright/light*
crème	*cream*
foncé(e)	*dark*
gris(e)	*grey*
jaune	*yellow*
marron	*brown*
noir(e)	*black*
noisette	*hazel*
orange	*orange*
pourpre	*purple (crimson)*
rose	*pink*
rouge	*red*
roux/rousse	*reddish/russet*
vert(e)	*green*
violet/violette	*purple*

Les dates (Dates)

Les jours de la semaine (Days of the week)

lundi	*Monday*
mardi	*Tuesday*
mercredi	*Wednesday*
jeudi	*Thursday*
vendredi	*Friday*
samedi	*Saturday*
dimanche	*Sunday*

l'an/l'année	*year*
le jour/la journée	*day*
le mois	*month*
une quinzaine (de jours)	*fortnight*
la semaine	*week*
le week-end	*weekend*

Les mois de l'année (Months of the year)

janvier	*January*
février	*February*
mars	*March*
avril	*April*
mai	*May*
juin	*June*
juillet	*July*
août	*August*
septembre	*September*
octobre	*October*
novembre	*November*
décembre	*December*

Les saisons (Seasons)

le printemps	*spring*
l'été (m)	*summer*
l'automne (m)	*autumn*
l'hiver (m)	*winter*

Les distances (Distances)

un centimètre	*one centimetre*
un kilomètre	*one kilometre*
un mètre	*one metre*

L'école (School)

Les écoles (Types of schools)

le collège (le CES : Collège d'Enseignement Secondaire)	*secondary school*
l'école maternelle (f)	*playschool*
l'école primaire (f)	*primary school*
la garderie	*crèche*
le lycée	*secondary school*
l'université (f)	*university*

À l'école (Around the school)

le bureau	*office*
la cantine	*canteen*
la cour	*yard*
le gymnase	*gymnasium/sports hall*
l'horloge (f)	*clock*
l'infirmerie (f)	*sick bay*
le laboratoire	*laboratory*
le/la professeur	*teacher*
la salle de classe	*classroom*
la salle des professeurs	*staffroom*
la salle d'informatique	*computer room*
la salle polyvalente	*all-purpose hall*
la sonnette	*bell*
le tableau d'affichage	*notice board*
le terrain de sports	*sports ground*
le vestiaire	*cloakroom*
l'instituteur/trice (m/f)	*primary school teacher*
le/la proviseur	*principal*
le proviseur adjoint	*deputy principal*
l'infirmier/ière (m/f)	*nurse*
le/la surveillant(e)	*supervisor*
le/la secrétaire	*secretary*
les toilettes (f)	*toilets*

La salle de classe (The classroom)

l'affiche (f)	*poster*
la brosse	*blackboard cleaner*
le bureau	*desk*
la carte	*map*
la chaise	*chair*
le cours	*class*
les étagères (f)	*shelves*
la fenêtre	*window*
le feutre	*marker*
le magnétophone	*taperecorder*

le magnétoscope	*video machine*
le mur	*wall*
l'ordinateur (m)	*computer*
le placard	*press*
le plafond	*ceiling*
le plancher	*floor*
la porte	*door*
la poubelle	*bin*
le projecteur	*projector*
le rétroprojecteur	*overhead projector*
le tableau	*board*
le tableau (noir/blanc)	*black/white board*

Le cartable (*Schoolbag*)

l'agenda (m)	*diary/school journal*
l'agrafeuse (f)	*stapler*
le cahier	*copy*
le carnet	*notebook*
le classeur	*folder*
le livre	*book*
la pochette	*plastic pocket*
le scotch	*sellotape*

La trousse (*Pencil case*)

la agrafeuse (f)	*stapler*
la colle	*glue*
la calculatrice	*calculator*
les ciseaux (m)	*scissors*
le compas	*compass*
le crayon	*pencil*
les crayons de couleurs	*coloured pencils*
le feutre	*marker*
la gomme	*eraser*
la règle	*ruler*
le surligneur fluo	*highlight pen*
le stylo	*biro*
le stylo correcteur	*correcting pen*
le taille-crayon	*sharpener*

Les matières (*School subjects*)

l'allemand (m)	*German*
l'anglais (m)	*English*
les arts ménagers (m)	*Home Economics*
les arts plastiques (m)	*Craftwork*
la biologie	*Biology*
la chimie	*Chemistry*
le commerce	*Business Studies*

la comptabilité	*Accounting*
le dessin	*Art/Drawing*
le dessin technique	*Technical Drawing*
l'éducation civique (f)	*CSPE*
l'éducation religieuse (f)	*Religion*
l'EPS (f)	*PE*
(Éducation Physique et Sportive)	
l'espagnol (m)	*Spanish*
le français	*French*
le gaélique/l'irlandais (m)	*Irish*
la géographie	*Geography*
le grec	*Greek*
l'histoire (f)	*History*
l'italien (m)	*Italian*
le latin	*Latin*
les maths (f)	*Maths*
la physique	*Physics*
la technologie	*Technology*
la menuiserie	*Woodwork*

La famille et les amis (*Family and friends*)

l'aîné(e) (m/f)	*oldest/eldest*
un/une ami(e)	*friend*
le beau-père	*step-father/ father-in-law*
la belle-mère	*step-mother/ mother-in-law*
le cadet/la cadette	*the youngest*
le/la camarade	*class-mate/ work-mate*
le copain/la copine	*friend/pal*
le/la cousin(e) (m/f)	*cousin*
l'épouse (f)	*wife*
l'époux (m)	*husband*
la femme	*wife*
la fille	*daughter*
le fils	*son*
le frère	*brother*
la grand-mère	*grandmother*
le grand-père	*grandfather*
le/les jumeau(x) (m)	*twin(s)*
la/les jumelle(s) (f)	*twin(s)*
la maman	*mammy/mum*
la mamie	*granny/nanny*
le mari	*husband*
la marraine	*godmother*
la mère	*mother*
le neveu	*nephew*

la nièce	niece
l'oncle (m)	uncle
le papa	daddy/dad
le papi	granddad
les parents	parents/relations
le parrain	godfather
le père	father
le petit ami	boyfriend
le petit-fils	grandson
la petite amie	girlfriend
la petite-fille	granddaughter
les petits-enfants	grandchildren
la sœur	sister
la tante	aunt
le/la voisin(e)	neighbour

Au garage (In the garage)

le capot	bonnet
le clignotant	indicator
le coffre	boot
conduire	to drive
démarrer	to move off
la dépanneuse	tow truck
essuyer	to wipe/clean
le frein à main	hand brake
les freins (m)	brakes
le klaxon	horn
le lave-auto	car wash
laver	to wash
l'essence (sans plomb) (f)	petrol (unleaded)
le moteur	engine
le pare-brise	windscreen
les phares (m)	head lights
la pompe	pump
le pompiste	petrol pump attendant
le pneu crevé	flat tyre
réparer	to repair
la roue	wheel
tomber en panne	to break down
le volant	steering wheel

Les gares et l'aéroport (m) (Stations and the airport)

l'accès aux quais (m)	entrance to platforms
l'aérogare (m)	airport terminal
l'ascenseur (m)	lift
le billet aller-retour	return ticket
le billet simple	single ticket

la billetterie automatique	automatic ticket-machine
le buffet	station restaurant
le chariot	trolley
Compostez vos billets !	Date-stamp your ticket!
la consigne	left luggage
la consigne automatique	luggage locker
les correspondances (f)	connections
l'entrée (f)	entrance
l'escalier roulant (m)	escalator
les horaires de train/bus	train/bus timetable
la gare (SNCF)	railway station
(Société Nationale des Chemins de Fer Français)	
la gare maritime	ferry terminal
la gare routière	bus station
le guichet	ticket-office/counter
la location de voitures	cars for hire
les objets trouvés (m)	lost property
le passage souterrain	underground walkway
la piste	runway
le point de rencontre	meeting place
la porte	door/gate
le quai	platform
les renseignements (m)	information
la salle d'attente	waiting room
la salle d'embarquement	boarding area
la sortie	exit
le tapis roulant	moving walkway
la zone fumeurs	smoking area
la zone non-fumeurs	non-smoking area

Les lieux (Places)

À la campagne (The countryside)

l'arbre (m)	tree
le bois	wood
le champ	field
la colline	hill
la fleur	flower
la forêt	forest
la haie	hedge
la montagne	mountain
le pré	meadow
la rivière	river
le ruisseau	stream

Au bord de la mer *(Seaside)*

le bateau	*boat*
le caillou	*pebble*
la falaise	*cliff*
le maître-nageur	*life guard*
la mer	*sea*
la mouette	*sea gull*
le parasol	*sunshade*
le paravent	*wind-break*
la pelle	*shovel*
le phare	*lighthouse*
la plage	*beach*
le port	*port*
le rocher	*rock*
le sable	*sand*
le seau	*bucket*
le transat	*deckchair*
la vague	*wave*
le voilier	*yacht*

En ville *(In town)*

le boulevard	*boulevard*
la déchetterie	*dump*
défense de jouer au foot	*playing football is forbidden*
défense de marcher sur la pelouse	*no walking on the grass*
les feux	*traffic lights*
l'immeuble (m)	*block of apartments*
le magasin	*shop*
le parc	*park*
le parc d'attractions	*theme park*
le parking	*carpark*
le parking municipal	*city/official carpark*
le passage clouté	*pedestrian crossing*
le passage souterrain	*subway*
la place	*square*
le pont	*bridge*
le réverbère	*street light/lamp-post*
la route	*road*
la rue	*road*
la ruelle	*alley/lane*
le trottoir	*path*
l'usine (f)	*factory*
le village	*village*
la ville	*town*
la zone industrielle	*industrial area*
la zone piétonne	*pedestrian area*

Les loisirs *(Pastimes)*

collectionner…	*to collect …*
… des timbres (m)	*… stamps*
… des pièces de monnaie (f)	*… coins*
… des pin's (m)	*… pins/badges*
… des porte-clés (m)	*… key-rings*
… des posters (m)	*… posters*
… des télécartes (f)	*… phone cards*
les jeux de société (m)	*board games*
les jeux vidéos (m)	*video games*
la lecture	*reading*
les échecs (m)	*chess*
faire des maquettes	*model-making*
les dames (f)	*checkers/draughts*
les mots croisés (m)	*crosswords*
la pêche	*fishing*
peindre	*to paint*
surfer sur le Net	*to surf the internet*
texter	*to text*
télécharger de la musique	*to download music*
tricoter	*knitting*

Les magasins et les bâtiments *(Shops and buildings)*

la banque	*bank*
la bibliothèque	*library*
la bijouterie	*jeweller's*
la boucherie	*butcher's*
la boulangerie	*bakery*
le café	*cafe*
le camping	*campsite*
la cathédrale	*cathedral*
le centre sportif	*sports centre*
la charcuterie	*pork butcher's*
la chocolaterie	*chocolate shop*
le cinéma	*cinema*
le club des jeunes	*youth club*
le/la coiffeur/euse	*barber/hairdresser*
la confiserie	*sweet shop*
la cour de justice	*court*
l'église (f)	*church*
la galerie	*gallery*
la gare	*station*
la gare routière	*bus station*
la gendarmerie	*police station*
l'hôpital (m)	*hospital*
l'hôtel de ville (m)	*town hall*

la librairie	book shop
la mairie	town hall
la Maison des Jeunes et de la Culture (MJC)	youth centre
la Maison de la Presse	newsagent
le marchand de chaussures	shoe shop
le marchand de fruits	fruit seller
le marchand de journaux	newsagent
la maroquinerie	leather goods shop
le musée	museum
l'office du tourisme (m)	tourist office
la papeterie	stationery shop
la pâtisserie	cake shop
la patinoire	skating rink
la pharmacie	chemist
le/la photographe	photographer
la piscine	swimming pool
la poste	post office
la quincaillerie	hardware shop
le restaurant	restaurant
le stade	stadium
la station-service	petrol station
le supermarché	supermarket
le syndicat d'initiative	tourist information office
le théâtre	theatre

Dans les magasins (In the shops)

l'accueil (m)	reception desk/area
l'ascenseur (m)	lift
la caisse	cash desk/check out
le/la caissier/ière	cashier
le comptoir	counter
l'électroménager (m)	household appliances
les produits congelés (m)	frozen goods
la promotion	special offer
la publicité	advertisement
le rayon	shelf
le reçu	receipt
le rez-de-chaussée	ground floor
la cabine (d'essayage)	fitting room
les soldes (m)	sales
le sous-sol	basement
le/la vendeur/euse	shop assistant
les produits biologiques (m)	organic produce
les produits artisanaux (m)	handcrafted/handmade products

La maison et le jardin (House and garden)

la balançoire	swing
la barrière	fence
le bassin	pond
la boîte aux lettres	letter box
la buanderie	utility room
le bureau	office
la cave	basement/cellar
la chambre	bedroom
la cuisine	kitchen
la douche	shower
l'escalier (m)	stairs
l'étage (m)	storey/floor
le grenier	attic
le jardin	garden
le palier	landing
la pièce	room
la remise	shed
la salle à manger	dining room
la salle de bains	bathroom
le salon	sitting room
le séjour	sitting room/living room
la serre	glasshouse
le sous-sol	basement
la terrasse	terrace/patio
les toilettes (f)	toilet
le toit	roof
la véranda	veranda/conservatory
le vestiaire	cloakroom
le vestibule	hall
les W.C. (m)	toilet

Les tissus et les matériaux (Fabric and materials)

l'argent (m)	silver
le bronze	bronze
carré(e)	check/checked
le coton	cotton
le cuir	leather
écossais	tartan
la laine	wool
l'or (m)	gold
une perle	pearl
à pois	spotted
rayé(e)	striped
la soie	silk
le tissu	fabric/cloth

Les meubles et les équipements (Furniture and equipment)

La chambre (Bedroom)

l'armoire (f)	wardrobe
la commode	chest of drawers
la couette	duvet cover
la couverture	blanket
le drap	sheet
l'étagère (f)	shelf
la lampe	lamp
le lit	bed
le miroir	mirror
l'oreiller (m)	pillow
le radio-réveil	radio-alarm-clock
le rayon	shelf
les rideaux	curtains
la table de nuit	bedside table
le tapis	carpet

La cuisine (Kitchen)

l'aspirateur (m)	hoover
l'assiette (f)	plate
le batteur électrique	beater
le bol	bowl
la bouilloire	kettle
la cafetière	coffee pot
la carafe	pitcher
la casserole	saucepan
la chaise	chair
le congélateur	freezer
le couteau	knife
la cuillère	spoon
la cuisinière	cooker
l'évier (m)	sink
le fer à repasser	iron
le four	oven
la fourchette	fork
le frigo	fridge
le lave-vaisselle	dish washer
la machine à laver	washing machine
le micro-onde	microwave
le placard	cupboard
la poêle	frying pan
le pot	jar
le robot mixeur	food mixer
le sucrier	sugar bowl
la table	table
la tasse	cup
le verre	glass

Le salon, le séjour et la salle à manger (Living room, sitting room and dining room)

la bibliothèque	bookshelves/bookcase
le buffet	sideboard
le canapé	sofa
la chaîne hi-fi	stereo system
le fauteuil	armchair
le lecteur CD	cd player
le magnétoscope	video
le tableau	painting
le téléviseur	television set

La salle de bains (Bathroom)

la baignoire	bath
la brosse à dents	tooth brush
la brosse à ongles	nail brush
le dentifrice	toothpaste
la douche	shower
le lavabo	hand-basin
les mouchoirs en papier	paper handkerchiefs
le papier hygiénique	toilet paper
le robinet	tap
le savon	soap
la serviette	towel
le shampoing	shampoo
la cuvette	toilet bowl
les W.C.	toilet

La musique (Music)

la batterie	drums
le/la chanteur/euse	singer
le chef d'orchestre	conductor
le clavier	keyboard
la clarinette	clarinet
la flûte à bec	recorder
la flûte irlandaise	tin whistle
le groupe	group
la guitare	guitar
le piano	piano
le tambour	drum
le tambourin	tambourine
la trompette	trumpet
l'orchestre (m)	orchestra
la chanson	song
les paroles (f)	words
le violon	violin
le violoncelle	cello

La nourriture (Food)

La viande (Meat)

l'agneau (m)	lamb
le bœuf	beef
le canard	duck
la côtelette	chop
la dinde	turkey
la volaille	poultry
le filet de…	filet of…
le foie	liver
le hamburger	hamburger
le jambon	ham
le lapin	rabbit
le mouton	mutton
le porc	pork
le poulet	chicken
le ragoût	stew
le rosbif	roast beef
le rôti de…	roast…
le saucisson	sausage
le steak	steak
le steak haché	minced steak
le veau	veal

Le poisson et les fruits de mer (Fish and seafood)

le cabillaud	cod
le carrelet	plaice
le crabe	crab
le homard	lobster
les huîtres (f)	oysters
les moules (f)	mussels
le saumon	salmon
la truite	trout
le thon	tuna

Les légumes (Vegetables)

l'artichaut (m)	artichoke
le brocoli	broccoli
les carottes (f)	carrots
le champignon	mushroom
le chou	cabbage
le chou-fleur	cauliflower
les choux de Bruxelles	Brussels sprouts
les épinards (m)	spinach
les haricots (m)	beans
les haricots verts (m)	French beans
la laitue	lettuce
le navet	turnip
l'oignon (m)	onion
le panais	parsnip
les petits pois (m)	peas
le poireau	leek
le poivron	pepper
la pomme de terre	potato

Les fruits (Fruits)

l'abricot (m)	apricot
l'ananas (m)	pineapple
la banane	banana
le cassis	blackcurrant
la cerise	cherry
le citron	lemon
le citron vert	lime
la fraise	strawberry
la framboise	raspberry
la groseille	gooseberry
le melon	melon
la mûre	blackberry
l'orange (f)	orange
le pamplemousse	grapefruit
la pêche	peach
la poire	pear
la pomme	apple
la prune	plum
le raisin	grape
le raisin sec	raisin
la tomate	tomato

Les ingrédients (Cookery ingredients)

le beurre	butter
la cannelle	cinnamon
la crème	cream
la crème fraîche	fresh cream
l'eau (f)	water
la farine	flour
le fromage	cheese
le gingembre	ginger
l'huile (f)	oil
le jus de citron	lemon juice
le lait	milk
le miel	honey
les miettes de pain (f)	bread crumbs
l'œuf (m)	egg
la pâte	pastry/paste

les pâtes (f)	pasta
le persil	parsley
le piment	chilli
le poivre	pepper
le sel	salt
le sucre	sugar

Les mesures (Measurements)

une boîte de	a tin of/a can of
une botte de	a small bunch of
une bouteille de	a bottle of/a jar of
un bouquet de	a bunch of
un brin de	a sprig of
un carton de	a box of
un centilitre de	a centilitre of
une cuillerée de	a spoon of
une cuillerée à café de	a teaspoon of
une cuillerée à soupe de	a tablespoon of
un demi-kilo de	a half-kilo of
un demi-litre de	a half-litre of
un gramme de	a gram of
une gousse de	a clove of
une livre de	a pound of
un kilo de	a kilo of
un litre de	a litre of
un paquet de	a packet of
une pincée de	a pinch of
un sachet de	a packet of/sachet of
une tasse de	a cup of
une tête de	a head of
une tranche de	a slice of

Les nouvelles technologies (New technologies)

allumer	to turn on
le blogue	blog
se brancher	to connect
le CDrom	CDrom
le clavier	keyboard
la clef USB	USB key
l'écran (m)	screen
envoyer un e-mail/ courriel	to send an email
éteindre	to turn off
le fichier	file
l'imprimante (f)	printer
l'ordinateur (m)	computer
l'ordinateur portable (m)	lap-top

l'oreillette (f)	earpiece
le parfeu	firewall
le réseau	network
surfer sur le Net	to surf the net
la souris	mouse
le texto	text message
texter	to text
les touches (f)	keys
taper	to type
télécharger	to download
un virus	virus

Les panneaux de signalisation (Roadside signs)

l'aire de jeux (f)	playground
l'aire de repos (f)	rest area/lay-by
Attention !	Watch out!
l'autoroute (f)	motorway
autres directions	other directions
le carrefour	crossroads
le centre-ville	town centre
défense de stationner	no parking
déviation	detour
le passage à niveau	level crossing
le péage	toll-booth
Ralentissez !	Slow down!
le rond-point	roundabout
une route bis	alternative route
un sens unique	one-way street
la sortie	exit
la sortie d'autoroute	motorway exit
la sortie de camions	lorry exit
la sortie de secours	emergency exit
la sortie d'usine	factory exit
sauf riverains	local access only
le stationnement	parking
stationnement interdit	no parking
toutes directions	all routes
des travaux	road works
Verglas fréquent !	Watch out for ice!
un virage dangereux	dangerous bend
une voie sans issue	cul-de-sac

Les pays (*Countries*)

l'Afrique (f)	*Africa*
l'Afrique du Sud (f)	*South Africa*
l'Algérie (f)	*Algeria*
l'Allemagne (f)	*Germany*
l'Angleterre (f)	*England*
l'Asie (f)	*Asia*
l'Australie (f)	*Australia*
l'Autriche (f)	*Austria*
la Belgique	*Belgium*
le Canada	*Canada*
la Chine	*China*
(l'île de) Chypre	*Cyprus*
la Croatie	*Croatia*
le Danemark	*Denmark*
l'Écosse (f)	*Scotland*
l'Espagne (f)	*Spain*
l'Estonie (f)	*Estonia*
les États-Unis	*America*
la Finlande	*Finland*
la France	*France*
la Grande-Bretagne	*Great Britain*
la Grèce	*Greece*
la Hongrie	*Hungary*
l'Irlande (f)	*Ireland*
l'Italie (f)	*Italy*
le Japon	*Japan*
la Lettonie	*Latvia*
la Lituanie	*Lithuania*
le Luxembourg	*Luxembourg*
le Maroc	*Morocco*
le Mexique	*Mexico*
la Norvège	*Norway*
les Pays-Bas	*Netherlands*
le Pays de Galles	*Wales*
la Pologne	*Poland*
le Portugal	*Portugal*
la République de Malte	*Malta*
la République Tchèque	*Czech Republic*
Le Royaume-Uni	*United Kingdom*
La Russie	*Russia*
la Slovaquie	*Slovakia*
la Slovénie	*Slovenia*
la Suède	*Sweden*
la Suisse	*Switzerland*
la Thaïlande	*Thailand*
la Tunisie	*Tunisia*
la Turquie	*Turkey*

Les professions/métiers (*Jobs*)

l'agriculteur/rice (m/f)	*farmer*
l'avocat(e) (m/f)	*lawyer*
le/la banquier/ière	*banker*
le/la batteur	*drummer*
le/la bibliothécaire	*librarian*
le/la boucher/ère	*butcher*
le/la boulanger/ère	*baker*
le/la chanteur/euse	*singer*
le/la charcutier/ière	*pork butcher*
le conducteur de bus	*bus driver*
le chauffeur de taxi	*taxi driver*
le/la chirurgien/ienne	*surgeon*
le/la coiffeur/euse	*hairdresser*
le/la comptable	*accountant*
le/la dentiste	*dentist*
l'électricien/ienne (m/f)	*electrician*
l'éleveur/euse (m/f)	*breeder*
l'esthéticienne (f)	*beautician*
le/la facteur/rice	*postman/postwoman*
le/la fermier/ière	*farmer*
le/la fonctionnaire	*civil servant*
le footballeur professionnel	*professional footballer*
le/la gérant(e)	*manager*
le gendarme	*police officer*
le/la guitariste	*guitarist*
l'homme d'affaires (m)	*businessman*
la femme d'affaires	*businesswoman*
l'informaticien/ienne (m/f)	*computer programmer*
l'agent immobilier (m/f)	*house agent*
l'infirmier/ière (m/f)	*nurse*
l'ingénieur (m/f)	*engineer*
l'instituteur/rice (m/f)	*primary school teacher*
le/la journaliste	*journalist*
le maçon	*bricklayer/builder*
le/la mannequin	*model*
le/la marchand(e) de journaux	*newspaper seller*
le/la mécanicien/ienne	*mechanic*
le médecin	*doctor*
le/la menuisier/ière	*carpenter*
le moniteur de ski	*ski instructor*
la monitrice de ski	*ski instructor*
le/la musicien/ienne	*musician*
le/la notaire	*solicitor*
l'ouvrier/ière (m/f)	*workman/ manual worker*
le/la pharmacien/ienne	*chemist*
le/la pilote	*pilot*

le d.j.	*D.J.*
le/la professeur	*teacher (second-level)*
le traiteur	*caterer*
la vedette	*star*
le/la vendeur/euse	*shop assistant*
le vétérinaire	*vet.*

Les sinistres et les accidents (disasters and accidents)

l'accident (m)	*accident*
l'avalanche (f)	*avalanche*
blessé(e)	*injured*
le cambriolage	*burglary*
le cambrioleur	*burglar*
la chute	*fall*
la collision	*collision*
le déraillement	*derailment*
le détournement	*hijacking*
le feu	*fire*
la grève	*strike*
le/la gréviste	*striker*
le hold-up	*hold-up*
l'incendie (m)	*fire*
l'inondation (f)	*flood*
le malfaiteur	*wrongdoer/criminal*
la manifestation	*protest march*
le meurtre	*murder*
la noyade	*drowning*
le naufrage	*shipwreck*
l'orage (m)	*storm*
l'otage (m)	*hostage*
l'ouragan (m)	*hurricane*
le raz-de-marée	*tsunami*
la sécheresse	*drought*
le séisme	*earthquake*
le sinistre	*disaster/catastrophe*
la tempête	*violent storm*
le tremblement de terre	*earthquake*
tué(e)	*killed*
la victime	*victim*
le vol	*theft/robbery*
le voleur	*thief/robber*

Les sports (Sports)

l'alpinisme (m)	*mountain climbing*
l'athlétisme (m)	*athletics*
l'aviron (m)	*rowing*
le canoë-kayak	*canoeing*
la boxe	*boxing*

l'équitation (f)	*horse-riding*
l'escalade (f)	*rock climbing*
l'escrime (f)	*fencing*
le footing	*jogging*
la lutte	*wrestling*
la natation	*swimming*
le patin à glace	*ice skating*
le patin à roulettes	*roller skating*
la planche à voile	*wind surfing*
la plongée	*diving*
la plongée sous-marine	*deep-sea diving*
la randonnée	*hiking*
le roller	*roller blading*
le saut en hauteur	*high jump*
le saut en longueur	*long jump*
le ski nautique	*water skiing*
le tir à l'arc	*archery*
le vélo	*cycling*
la voile	*sailing*

Le temps (Weather)

le beau temps	*fine weather*
le brouillard	*fog*
la bruine	*drizzle*
la brume	*mist*
brumeux/euse	*misty*
chaud(e)	*warm*
la chute de…	*fall of…*
couvert(e)	*overcast*
des éclaircies (f)	*bright/sunny spells*
les éclairs (m)	*lightning*
ensoleillé(e)	*sunny*
froid(e)	*cold*
le gel	*frost*
le mauvais temps	*bad weather*
la neige	*snow*
le nuage	*cloud*
nuageux/euse	*cloudy*
l'orage (m)	*storm*
orageux/euse	*stormy*
il pleut	*it is raining*
la pluie	*rain*
pluvieux/euse	*rainy*
la rafale	*gust of wind*
sec/sèche	*dry*
le soleil	*sun*
la tempête	*storm*
le tonnerre	*thunder*
le vent	*wind*
le verglas	*ice*

Les transports (Transport)

l'autobus (m)	*bus*
l'avion (m)	*airplane*
le bateau	*boat*
le bus	*bus*
le camion	*truck/lorry*
la camionnette	*van*
le car	*coach*
le car scolaire	*school bus*
le ferry	*ferry*
le funiculaire	*ski lift*
le métro	*underground*
la moto	*motorbike*
la navette	*shuttle bus/launch*
le pétrolier	*oil tanker*
le poids lourd	*heavy goods vehicle*
le remonte-pente	*ski lift*
la remorque	*trailer*
le TGV (Train à Grande Vitesse)	*express train*
le taxi	*taxi*
le tracteur	*tractor*
le train	*train*
le véhicule	*vehicle*
le vélo	*bicycle*
la voiture	*car*

Les vêtements et les accessoires (Clothes and accessories)

la bague	*ring*
les bas	*stockings*
les baskets (f)	*runners*
les bijoux (m)	*jewellery*
le blouson	*short jacket*
le bonnet	*swimming-cap*
la boucle d'oreille	*earring*
le bracelet	*bracelet*
les bottes (f)	*boots*
les bretelles (f)	*braces/shoulder straps*
la capuche	*hood*
la casquette	*cap*
la ceinture	*belt*
les chaussettes (f)	*socks*
les chaussures (f)	*shoes*
la chemise	*shirt/blouse*
le chemisier	*blouse*
le collant	*tights*
le collier	*necklace*

le complet/costume	*suit*
la cravate	*tie*
l'écharpe (f)	*scarf*
les gants (m)	*gloves*
le gilet à fermeture éclair	*zipped jacket*
le haut	*top*
l'imperméable (m)	*raincoat*
le jean	*jeans*
la jupe	*skirt*
le k-way	*rain-jacket*
le maillot	*football jersey/singlet*
le maillot de bain	*swimsuit*
le manteau	*coat*
la montre	*watch*
le pantalon	*trousers*
le portable	*mobile phone*
le portefeuille	*wallet*
le porte-monnaie	*purse*
le pull	*jumper*
le pyjama	*pyjamas*
la robe	*dress*
la robe de chambre	*nightdress*
le ruban	*ribbon*
le sac à main	*handbag*
le sac à dos	*rucksack*
les sandales (f)	*sandals*
le short	*shorts*
le survêtement	*tracksuit*
le tablier	*apron*
les talons (m)	*high heels*
le tee-shirt	*t-shirt*
les tongs (f)	*flip-flops*
la trousse de maquillage	*make-up purse*
la veste	*jacket*

Verb Table

aller — to go

	Présent	Imparfait	Passé composé	Futur	Conditionnel
je	vais	allais	suis allé(e)	irai	irais
tu	vas	allais	es allé(e)	iras	irais
il/elle/on	va	allait	il/on est allé	ira	irait
elle			est allée		
nous	allons	allions	sommes allé(e)s	irons	irions
vous	allez	alliez	êtes allé(e)(s)	irez	iriez
ils	vont	allaient	sont allés	iront	iraient
elles			sont allées		

avoir — to have

	Présent	Imparfait	Passé composé	Futur	Conditionnel
j'	ai	avais	ai eu	aurai	aurais
tu	as	avais	as eu	auras	aurais
il/elle/on	a	avait	a eu	aura	aurait
nous	avons	avions	avons eu	aurons	aurions
vous	avez	aviez	avez eu	aurez	auriez
ils/elles	ont	avaient	ont eu	auront	auraient

boire — to drink

	Présent	Imparfait	Passé composé	Futur	Conditionnel
je	bois	buvais	ai bu	boirai	boirais
tu	bois	buvais	as bu	boiras	boirais
il/elle/on	boit	buvait	a bu	boira	boirait
nous	buvons	buvions	avons bu	boirons	boirions
vous	buvez	buviez	avez bu	boirez	boiriez
ils/elles	boivent	buvaient	ont bu	boiront	boiraient

comprendre — to understand

	Présent	Imparfait	Passé composé	Futur	Conditionnel
je	comprends	comprenais	ai compris	comprendrai	comprendrais
tu	comprends	comprenais	as compris	comprendras	comprendrais
il/elle/on	comprend	comprenait	a compris	comprendra	comprendrait
nous	comprenons	comprenions	avons compris	comprendrons	comprendrions
vous	comprenez	compreniez	avez compris	comprendrez	comprendriez
ils/elles	comprennent	comprenaient	ont compris	comprendront	comprendraient

connaître — to know (people, places)

	Présent	Imparfait	Passé composé	Futur	Conditionnel
je	connais	connaissais	ai connu	connaîtrai	connaîtrais
tu	connais	connaissais	as connu	connaîtras	connaîtrais
il/elle/on	connaît	connaissait	a connu	connaîtra	connaîtrait
nous	connaissons	connaissions	avons connu	connaîtrons	connaîtrions
vous	connaissez	connaissiez	avez connu	connaîtrez	connaîtriez
ils/elles	connaissent	connaissaient	ont connu	connaîtront	connaîtraient

devoir — to have to (must)

	Présent	Imparfait	Passé composé	Futur	Conditionnel
je	dois	devais	ai dû	devrai	devrais
tu	dois	devais	as dû	devras	devrais
il/elle/on	doit	devait	a dû	devra	devrait
nous	devons	devions	avons dû	devrons	devrions
vous	devez	deviez	avez dû	devrez	devriez
ils/elles	doivent	devaient	ont dû	devront	devraient

Infinitif: dire — to say, to tell

	Présent	Imparfait	Passé composé	Futur	Conditionnel
je/j'	dis	disais	ai dit	dirai	dirais
tu	dis	disais	as dit	diras	dirais
il/elle/on	dit	disait	a dit	dira	dirait
nous	disons	disions	avons dit	dirons	dirions
vous	dites	disiez	avez dit	direz	diriez
ils/elles	disent	disaient	ont dit	diront	diraient

Infinitif: écrire — to write

	Présent	Imparfait	Passé composé	Futur	Conditionnel
je/j'	écris	écrivais	ai écrit	écrirai	écrirais
tu	écris	écrivais	as écrit	écriras	écrirais
il/elle/on	écrit	écrivait	a écrit	écrira	écrirait
nous	écrivons	écrivions	avons écrit	écrirons	écririons
vous	écrivez	écriviez	avez écrit	écrirez	écririez
ils/elles	écrivent	écrivaient	ont écrit	écriront	écriraient

Infinitif: envoyer — to send

	Présent	Imparfait	Passé composé	Futur	Conditionnel
je/j'	envoie	envoyais	ai envoyé	enverrai	enverrais
tu	envoies	envoyais	as envoyé	enverras	enverrais
il/elle/on	envoie	envoyait	a envoyé	enverra	enverrait
nous	envoyons	envoyions	avons envoyé	enverrons	enverrions
vous	envoyez	envoyiez	avez envoyé	enverrez	enverriez
ils/elles	envoient	envoyaient	ont envoyé	enverront	enverraient

Infinitif: être — to be

	Présent	Imparfait	Passé composé	Futur	Conditionnel
je/j'	suis	étais	ai été	serai	serais
tu	es	étais	as été	seras	serais
il/elle/on	est	était	a été	sera	serait
nous	sommes	étions	avons été	serons	serions
vous	êtes	étiez	avez été	serez	seriez
ils/elles	sont	étaient	ont été	seront	seraient

Infinitif: faire — to do, to make

	Présent	Imparfait	Passé composé	Futur	Conditionnel
je/j'	fais	faisais	ai fait	ferai	ferais
tu	fais	faisais	as fait	feras	ferais
il/elle/on	fait	faisait	a fait	fera	ferait
nous	faisons	faisions	avons fait	ferons	ferions
vous	faites	faisiez	avez fait	ferez	feriez
ils/elles	font	faisaient	ont fait	feront	feraient

Infinitif: lire — to read

	Présent	Imparfait	Passé composé	Futur	Conditionnel
je/j'	lis	lisais	ai lu	lirai	lirais
tu	lis	lisais	as lu	liras	lirais
il/elle/on	lit	lisait	a lu	lira	lirait
nous	lisons	lisions	avons lu	lirons	lirions
vous	lisez	lisiez	avez lu	lirez	liriez
ils/elles	lisent	lisaient	ont lu	liront	liraient

mettre — to put

	Présent	Imparfait	Passé composé	Futur	Conditionnel
je/j'	mets	mettais	ai mis	mettrai	mettrais
tu	mets	mettais	as mis	mettras	mettrais
il/elle/on	met	mettait	a mis	mettra	mettrait
nous	mettons	mettions	avons mis	mettrons	mettrions
vous	mettez	mettiez	avez mis	mettrez	mettriez
ils/elles	mettent	mettaient	ont mis	mettront	mettraient

partir — to leave, to depart

	Présent	Imparfait	Passé composé	Futur	Conditionnel
je	pars	partais	suis parti(e)	partirai	partirais
tu	pars	partais	es parti(e)	partiras	partirais
il/on	part	partait	est parti	partira	partirait
elle			est partie		
nous	partons	partions	sommes parti(e)s	partirons	partirions
vous	partez	partiez	êtes parti(e)(s)	partirez	partiriez
ils	partent	partaient	sont partis	partiront	partiraient
elles			sont parties		

pleuvoir — to rain

	Présent	Imparfait	Passé composé	Futur	Conditionnel
il	pleut	pleuvait	a plu	pleuvra	pleuvrait

pouvoir — to be able to

	Présent	Imparfait	Passé composé	Futur	Conditionnel
je/j'	peux	pouvais	ai pu	pourrai	pourrais
tu	peux	pouvais	as pu	pourras	pourrais
il/elle/on	peut	pouvait	a pu	pourra	pourrait
nous	pouvons	pouvions	avons pu	pourrons	pourrions
vous	pouvez	pouviez	avez pu	pourrez	pourriez
ils/elles	peuvent	pouvaient	ont pu	pourront	pourraient

prendre — to take

	Présent	Imparfait	Passé composé	Futur	Conditionnel
je/j'	prends	prenais	ai pris	prendrai	prendrais
tu	prends	prenais	as pris	prendras	prendrais
il/elle/on	prend	prenait	a pris	prendra	prendrait
nous	prenons	prenions	avons pris	prendrons	prendrions
vous	prenez	preniez	avez pris	prendrez	prendriez
ils/elles	prennent	prenaient	ont pris	prendront	prendraient

recevoir — to get, to receive

	Présent	Imparfait	Passé composé	Futur	Conditionnel
je/j'	reçois	recevais	ai reçu	recevrai	recevrais
tu	reçois	recevais	as reçu	recevras	recevrais
il/elle/on	reçoit	recevait	a reçu	recevra	recevrait
nous	recevons	recevions	avons reçu	recevrons	recevrions
vous	recevez	receviez	avez reçu	recevrez	recevriez
ils/elles	reçoivent	recevaient	ont reçu	recevront	recevraient

savoir — to know (information, knowledge)

	Présent	Imparfait	Passé composé	Futur	Conditionnel
je / j'	sais	savais	ai su	saurai	saurais
tu	sais	savais	as su	sauras	saurais
il/elle/on	sait	savait	a su	saura	saurait
nous	savons	savions	avons su	saurons	saurions
vous	savez	saviez	avez su	saurez	sauriez
ils/elles	savent	savaient	ont su	sauront	sauraient

sortir — to go out

	Présent	Imparfait	Passé composé	Futur	Conditionnel
je	sors	sortais	suis sorti(e)	sortirai	sortirais
tu	sors	sortais	es sorti(e)	sortiras	sortirais
il/on	sort	sortait	est sorti	sortira	sortirait
elle			est sortie		
nous	sortons	sortions	sommes sorti(e)s	sortirons	sortirions
vous	sortez	sortiez	êtes sorti(e)(s)	sortirez	sortiriez
ils	sortent	sortaient	sont sortis	sortiront	sortiraient
elles			sont sorties		

tenir — to hold

	Présent	Imparfait	Passé composé	Futur	Conditionnel
je / j'	tiens	tenais	ai tenu	tiendrai	tiendrais
tu	tiens	tenais	as tenu	tiendras	tiendrais
il/elle/on	tient	tenait	a tenu	tiendra	tiendrait
nous	tenons	tenions	avons tenu	tiendrons	tiendrions
vous	tenez	teniez	avez tenu	tiendrez	tiendriez
ils/elles	tiennent	tenaient	ont tenu	tiendront	tiendraient

venir — to come

	Présent	Imparfait	Passé composé	Futur	Conditionnel
je	viens	venais	suis venu(e)	viendrai	viendrais
tu	viens	venais	es venu(e)	viendras	viendrais
il/on	vient	venait	est venu	viendra	viendrait
elle			est venue		
nous	venons	venions	sommes venu(e)s	viendrons	viendrions
vous	venez	veniez	êtes venu(e)(s)	viendrez	viendriez
ils	viennent	venaient	sont venus	viendront	viendraient
elles			sont venues		

voir — to see

	Présent	Imparfait	Passé composé	Futur	Conditionnel
je / j'	vois	voyais	ai vu	verrai	verrais
tu	vois	voyais	as vu	verras	verrais
il/elle/on	voit	voyait	a vu	verra	verrait
nous	voyons	voyions	avons vu	verrons	verrions
vous	voyez	voyiez	avez vu	verrez	verriez
ils/elles	voient	voyaient	ont vu	verront	verraient

vouloir — to want, to wish

	Présent	Imparfait	Passé composé	Futur	Conditionnel
je / j'	veux	voulais	ai voulu	voudrai	voudrais
tu	veux	voulais	as voulu	voudras	voudrais
il/elle/on	veut	voulait	a voulu	voudra	voudrait
nous	voulons	voulions	avons voulu	voudrons	voudrions
vous	voulez	vouliez	avez voulu	voudrez	voudriez
ils/elles	veulent	voulaient	ont voulu	voudront	voudraient

The Night Before the Exam

- Stay calm!
- Don't panic!
- Be positive!
- You probably will know much more than you think!

Remember…

- Look over a **sample paper** so that you are familiar with what you are going to be doing tomorrow. You could use the **Exam Paper Analysis 2009**, which is included on pages 110/131 in this book
- Take each section in turn, i.e. Listening Comprehension, Reading Comprehension and Written Expression sections
- Listen to **one or two tracks from your CD** to remind yourself of what type of question you can expect to hear
- Pay particular attention to the **Points to note** boxes
- Remind yourself of the type of question which you will have to read on the Reading Comprehension section of the paper, i.e. ads, recipes, newspaper articles and interviews
- Don't forget to revise the **layout** for the various types of Written Expression exercises, i.e. informal letters, formal letters, postcards, messages, notes, faxes and emails
- Revise the **main tenses** needed when writing
- Don't forget the **phrases** for beginning and ending your two pieces of writing
- Revise some key **phrases** for postcards and messages

Bonne chance !

Date

Time

Section to
be revised

Date

Time

Section to
be revised

Date

Time

Section to
be revised

Date

Time

Section to
be revised

Date

Time

Section to
be revised

Date

Time

Section to
be revised

Night before exam

Sections to
be revised

Date

Time

Section to
be revised

Date

Time

Section to
be revised

Date

Time

Section to
be revised

Date

Time

Section to
be revised

Date

Time

Section to
be revised

Date

Time

Section to
be revised

Night before exam

Sections to
be revised

Date			
Time			
Section to be revised			

Date			
Time			
Section to be revised			

Date			
Time			
Section to be revised			

Date			
Time			
Section to be revised			

Date			
Time			
Section to be revised			

Date			
Time			
Section to be revised			

Night before exam	
Sections to be revised	

Date

Time

Section to
be revised

Date

Time

Section to
be revised

Date

Time

Section to
be revised

Date

Time

Section to
be revised

Date

Time

Section to
be revised

Date

Time

Section to
be revised

Night before exam

Sections to
be revised